KEYISSUES

Problem Solving

Supporting Problem Solving skills in young learners

Written by MARGARET MARTIN
Edited by SALLY FEATHERSTONE

Revised edition published 2013 by Featherstone Education
Bloomsbury Publishing plc
50 Bedford Square, London,
www.bloomsbury.com

First Published 2007 by Featherstone

ISBN 978-1-4081-8690-9

Grateful thanks are offered to TTS Group Ltd, who have provided several of the images used in this publication.

Thanks to Wendy C., Sue F. and Brian M.

A CIP record for this publication is available from the British Library.

Printed and bound in India by Replika Press Pvt. Ltd

This book is produced using paper that is made from wood grown in managed, sustainable forests. It is natural, renewable and recyclable. The logging and manufacturing processes conform to the environmental regulations of the country of origin.

To see our full range of titles visit **www.bloomsbury.com**

CONTENTS

PART 1 INTRODUCTION 5
- About this book
- About Problem Solving

Problem Solving in the curriculum 8
- Problem Solving and Mathematics
- Links to the Foundation Stage in England
- Links to the Foundation Stage in Scotland
- Links to the Foundation Stage in Northern Ireland
- Links to the Foundation Stage in Wales

The environment for Problem Solving 13
- Ten tips for creating a Problem Solving environment
- Resources
- Asking questions

Effective planning for Problem Solving 13
- Encouraging Problem Solving skills in every day activities
- Involving children in planning
- Building Problem Solving into your continuous provision
- Making opportunities to practise Problem Solving
- Building Problem Solving into your planned activities for groups and individuals
- Involving parents and carers in Problem Solving

PART 2 PLANNED PROBLEM SOLVING ACTIVITIES 21

ART/DESIGN 24
- Make a bag
- A Small World castle
- Scary Mask!

COMMUNICATION AND LANGUAGE 28
- Bear Hunt
- Animal Rhyme
- Funny Story

CONSTRUCTION 32
- Giraffe House
- Boat Building
- Buggy or Trolley?

MATHEMATICS 36
- Glueless Person
- What a Mix-up!
- A Piece of Cake

MUSIC/SOUND-MAKING 40
Happy Music
Scary Sounds
Making Music

PHYSICAL DEVELOPMENT 44
Hungry Crocodile
Obstacle Course
Fast Dance

SAND AND WATER PLAY 48
Small World Toys
Wet Sand
Tall Building
Stop the Leak!
Empty the Tray
Pirate Treasure

SCIENCE/INVESTIGATION 56
Toy Car
Beads and Balls
Giant Bubbles

TECHNOLOGY 60
Remote-Controlled Car
Mending Games
Bee-Bot

WRITING 64
Bear Hunt 2
Tiny Birthday
Lunch Menu

OUTDOOR PLAY 68
Bird House
Game for this Picture
Make a Den!
Waterway
Teddy Cool

RESOURCES 75

PROBLEM SOLVING BANK 78

Part 1

INTRODUCTION

The problem of the twenty pound note

Think about this problem, which might happen to you:

A £20 note has fallen down the gap between the cooker and a fixed kitchen unit. How would you solve the problem of getting it back?

Would you:

- try to poke it out using a tool such as a ruler or stick?
- adapt something to make a tool, such as bending a wire coat hanger?
- try to stick it to something like Blu Tack or double-sided sellotape on a garden cane?
- attempt to suck it out using a vacuum cleaner, with or without a pop sock or tissue on the end to stop it disappearing into the dust bag?
- try to lever the cooker up using a strong metal implement so you can reach it by hand or tool?
- ask someone to help you?
- decide it's impossible or not important, and forget about it until you are replacing the cooker or kitchen units?
- think of some other way?

What are the skills, knowledge and concepts you need to call on to reach your decision? The answers may give you some insight into the benefits of using a Problem Solving approach when working with children.

ABOUT THIS BOOK

This book is for practitioners working with young children in schools, nurseries, playgroups, informal groups and at home. It is intended to help provide and structure Problem Solving.

This book aims to help practitioners in the following ways:

- Providing information about Problem Solving
- Looking at the existing practice within the setting
- Help in auditing resources and equipment by checking against the suggestion lists
- Help in sourcing less common resources
- Providing suggestions for everyday Problem Solving, including the involvement of children in the planning process
- Providing a bank of activities which allows the practitioner to plan for Problem Solving across the curriculum
- Giving ideas for creating a variety of stimuli to present Problem Solving to the children
- Providing suggestion for involving parents and carers in supporting Problem Solving at home.

Although it is one of the Key Issues series of books aimed at supporting practitioners in England using the Early Years Foundation Stage curriculum, it will also be of use to staff following the Scottish Curriculum for Excellence, the Welsh Foundation Phase curriculum and the Foundation Stage curriculum in Northern Ireland.

ABOUT PROBLEM SOLVING

There are a number of definitions of Problem Solving, and they all link the ability to solve problems with the range of Thinking Skills. The skill of Problem Solving engages us in building on known concepts, knowledge and previous experience and using these in new ways to find solutions and answers which may not at first seem obvious.

Problem Solving is not an activity with a defined product or outcome at the end, but rather **a process**. At the end of the process, a child, or group of children, might conclude, based on what they know and can do at the time, that there is no solution to the problem. Of course, as we get older, and our experience increases, we can often solve problems that seemed to be insoluble before.

Thinking is of prime importance in Problem Solving. Children should be encouraged to think creatively and use their imagination, and the key to developing thinking lies in the development of language. The ability to use **language** for thinking is an essential and unique human ability. Children need the vocabulary of:

nouns – to name the resources and materials they are working with

adjectives – to describe what something looks, sounds, tastes, feels or smells like

verbs – to describe the actions that they, others and objects make

adverbs – to add value to the verbs they use

prepositions – for positional language.

The six Thinking Skills are:

- enquiry
- information processing
- reasoning
- evaluation
- Problem Solving
- creativity

Within a design challenge, Problem Solving can be used to describe a number of approaches the learners may adopt. These could include investigative approaches, trial and error, visualisation, breaking the problem into smaller components, collaberation with others and appropriate strategies.

Appendix – Explanations, Scottish Curriculum for Excellence

Language allows children to negotiate and interact with others they work with. Language also helps children to organise, sequence and clarify their thinking so they can reply to open-ended questions posed by practitioners and other adults.

Well developed language also allows children to negotiate and interact with others as they work.

Young children can solve problems, and by challenging, supporting and extending their thinking on a regular basis, this skill will develop and become a permanent feature of their learning, especially if the problems we pose are meaningful and relevant to the children's interests.

Problem Solving approaches can be used in all areas of the curriculum. The process can happen informally in the everyday life of the setting, in independent and child-initiated activities, or can be incorporated into planned activities and experiences.

This book is intended to support practitioners in providing a Problem Solving approach and building it in to their practice.

> *'When children have opportunities to play with ideas in different situations and with a variety of resources, they discover connections and come to new and better understandings and ways of doing things. Adult support in this process enhances their ability to think critically and ask questions.'*
>
> **Early Years Foundation Stage Guidance**

PROBLEM SOLVING IN THE CURRICULUM

PROBLEM SOLVING AND MATHEMATICS

Here is what the EYFS says about Problem Solving in the curriculum:

'The Statutory Framework for the Early Years Foundation Stage, states: 'Mathematics involves providing children with opportunities to develop and improve their skills in counting, understanding and using numbers, calculating simple addition and subtraction problems; and to describe shapes, spaces and measures.'

'Mathematics is important in our everyday life, allowing us to make sense of the world around us and to manage our lives. Using mathematics enables us to model real-life situations and make connections and informed prediction. It equips us with the skills we need to interpret and analyse information, simplify and solve problems, assess risk and make informed decisions.'

'From the early stages onwards, children and young people should experience success in mathematics and develop the confidence to take risks, ask questions and explore alternative solutions without fear of being wrong. They will enjoy exploring and applying mathematical concepts to understand and solve problems, explaining their thinking and presenting their solutions to others in a variety of ways.'

'Mathematics is at its most powerful when the knowledge and understanding that have been developed are used to solve problems. Problem Solving will be at the heart of all our learning and teaching.'

Principles and practice, Curriculum for Excellence, Scotland

'Mathematics will be more practical so that children can see how problems are solved and how important mathematics is in their everyday lives. There will be more emphasis on children understanding how things work and on finding different ways to solve problems.'

Foundation Phase introduction, Wales

'Children should develop their application and understanding of their mathematical skills using contexts and techniques from across the range. They should be given opportunities to –

Solve mathematical problems:

- select and use appropriate ideas, equipment and materials to solve practical problems.

Communicate mathematically:

- develop their mathematical language across the range of areas and use it in their role play and in communicating/talking to adults about their work.'

Framework for Children's Learning for 3 to 7-year-olds in Wales

'Children will acquire early mathematical concepts through activities that involve sorting, matching, comparing, classifying, and making patterns and sequences in a variety of contexts. These activities should involve children playing, exploring and investigating, doing and observing, talking and listening and asking and answering questions'

Foundation Stage, Northern Ireland

LINKS TO THE FOUNDATION STAGE IN ENGLAND

The EYFS states – 'In planning and guiding children's activities, practitioners must reflect on the different ways that children learn and reflect these in their practices. Three characteristics of effective teaching and learning are :

- Playing and exploring – children investigate and experience things, and "have a go"
- Active learning – children concentrate and keep on trying if they encounter difficulties, and enjoy achievements
- Creating and thinking critically – children have and develop their own ideas, make links between ideas, and develop strategies for doing things'

The 7 curricular areas are divided into prime and specific areas:

Prime areas

Communication and language

Physical Development

Personal, social and emotional development

Specific areas

Literacy

Mathematics

Understanding the world

Expressive arts and design

Through the planned Problem Solving activities in this book, children will be supported in the development of the following Early Learning Goals. Other goals will also be supported, but less directly.

PHYSICAL DEVELOPMENT

Moving and handling: children show good control and co-ordination in large and small movements. They move confidently in a range of ways, safely negotiating space. They handle equipment and tools effectively, including pencils for writing.

LITERACY

Reading: children read and understand simple sentences. They use phonic knowledge to decode regular words and read them aloud accurately. They also read some common irregular words. They demonstrate understanding when talking with others about what they have read.

Writing: children use their phonic knowledge to write words in ways which match their spoken sounds. They also write some irregular common words. They write simple sentences which can be read by themselves and others. Some words are spelt correctly and others are phonetically plausible.

MATHEMATICS

Numbers: children count reliably with numbers 1 to 20, place them in order and say which number is one more or one less than a given number, Using quantities and objects, they add and subtract two single-digit numbers and count on or back to find the answer. They solve problems, including doubling, halving and sharing.

Shape, space and measure: children use everyday language to talk about size, weight, capacity, position, distance, time and money to compare quantities and objects and to solve problems. They recognise, create and describe patterns. They explore characteristics of everyday objects and shapes and use mathematical language to describe them.

UNDERSTANDING THE WORLD

The world: children know about similarities and differences in relation to places, objects, materials and living things. They talk about the features of their own immediate environment and how environments might vary from one another. They make observations of animals and plants and explain why some things occur, and talk about changes.

Technology: children recognise that a range of technology is used in places such as homes and schools. They select and use technology for particular purposes.

EXPRESSIVE ARTS

Exploring and using media and materials: children sing songs, make music and dance, and experiment with ways of changing them. They safely use and explore a variety of materials, tools and techniques, experimenting with colour, design, texture, form and function.

Being imaginative: children use what they have learnt about media and materials in original ways, thinking about uses and purposes. They represent their own ideas, thoughts and feelings through design and technology, art, music, dance, role play and stories.

LINKS TO THE FOUNDATION STAGE IN SCOTLAND

The Curriculum for Excellence (CfE) in Scotland was adopted in August 2010 and is intended to provide a broad general education from the early years to the end of S3.

There are 8 curricular areas:

Expressive Arts (EXA)

Health and Wellbeing (HWB)

Languages and Literacy (LIT)

Mathematics and Numeracy (MNU)

Religious and Moral Education (RME)

Sciences (SCN)

Social Studies (SOC)

Technologies (TCH)

The following introductory statements of experiences and outcomes for the Early Level are those most relevant to the planned Problem Solving activities within this book. Other areas will also be developed, but less directly.

EXPRESSIVE ARTS

EXA 0-02a: I have the freedom to discover and choose ways to create images and objects using a variety of materials.

EXA 0-05a: Inspired by a range of stimuli, I can express and communicate my ideas, thoughts and feelings through activities within art and design.

EXA 0-06a: Working on my own and with others, I use my curiosity and imagination to solve design problems.

EXA 0-17a: I have the freedom to use my voice, musical instruments and music technology to discover and enjoy playing with sound and rhythm.

EXA 0-18a: Inspired by a range of stimuli, and working on my own/or with others, I can express and communicate my ideas, thoughts and feelings through musical activities.

LANGUAGES AND LITERACY

LIT0-01a/LIT 0-11a/LIT 0-20a: I enjoy exploring and playing with the patterns and sounds of language and can use what I learn.

LIT 0-09b/LIT 0-19a/LIT 0-31a: I enjoy exploring events and characters in stories and other texts and I use what I learn to invent my own, sharing these with others in imaginative ways.

LIT 0-21b: As I play and learn, I enjoy exploring interesting materials for writing and different ways of recording my experiences and feelings, ideas and information.

MATHEMATICS

MNU 0-01a: I am developing a sense of size and amount by observing, exploring, using and communicating with others about things in the world around me.

MNU 0-02a: I have explored numbers, understanding that they represent quantities and I can use them to count, create sequences and describe order.

MNU 0-07a: I can share out a group of items by making smaller groups and can split a whole object into smaller parts.

MNU 0-20b: I can match objects, and sort using my own and others' criteria, sharing my ideas with others.

SCIENCES

SCN 0-07a: Through everyday experiences and play with a variety of toys and other objects, I can recognise simple types of forces and describe their effects.

SCN 0-11a: Through play, I have explored a variety of ways of making sounds.

SCN 0-15a: Through creative play, I explore different materials and can share my reasoning for selecting materials for different purposes.

TECHNOLOGIES

TCH 0-0-1a: I enjoy playing with and exploring technologies to discover what they can do and how they can help us.

TCH 0-0-9a: I am developing Problem Solving strategies, navigation and co-ordination skills, as I play and learn with electronic games, remote control or programmable toys.

TCH 0-11a: Throughout my learning, I share my thoughts with others to help further develop ideas and solve problems.

TCH 0-12a: Within real and imaginary settings, I am developing my practical skills as I select and work with a range of materials, tools and software.

TCH 0-14a: Through discovery, natural curiosity and imagination, I explore ways to construct models or solve problems.

TCH 0-15a: Throughout my learning, I explore different ways of representing my ideas in imaginative ways.

LINKS TO THE FOUNDATION STAGE IN NORTHERN IRELAND

The Foundation Stage has 7 Areas of Learning:

LL – Language and Literacy (including Talking and Listening, Reading and Writing)

MN – Mathematics and Numeracy (including Number, Measures, Shape and Space, Sorting and Patterns and Relationships)

A – The Arts (including Art and Design, Music and Drama)

WAU – The World Around Us

PDMU – Personal Development and Mutual Understanding (including Personal Understanding and Health and Mutual Understanding in the Local and Wider Community)

PDM – Physical Development and Movement

RE – Religious Education

Through using the planned Problem Solving activities in this book, knowledge, understanding and skills will be developed in the following Areas of Learning. Other Areas will also be developed, but less directly.

LANGUAGE AND LITERACY

Talking and listening

- identifying and generating rhymes
- talking about their work, play and things they have made

Writing

- distinguish between writing and drawing
- understand that writing is a means of communication and can be used for
- different purposes
- write in a range of genres with teacher guidance (Progression)

MATHEMATICS AND NUMERACY

Understanding number -

- count a variety of objects
- explore the number that comes after, before, between a given number

Measures

- compare two objects of different length/weight/capacity/area; understand and use the language of comparison

Shape and Space

- build and make models with 3D shapes; create pictures and patterns with 2D shapes
- describe and name common 2D and 3D shapes

Sorting

- explore freely properties of a range of materials and one/two/three property collections; respond to questions about the arrangement

Progression in MN

- recognise numbers to at least 20
- begin to measure using non-standard units
- be involved in solving practical problems

THE ARTS

Art and Design

- explore and use a wide range of materials and processes

Progression in Art and Design

- explore and discover qualities of various materials in order to make choices and to create their own unique pictures and structures
- begin to develop a range of skills using materials, tools and processes (drawing, painting, printmaking, textiles, malleable materials and three dimensional construction)

Music

- work creatively with sound

Progression in Music

- make music

Drama

- express thoughts, ideas and feelings

THE WORLD AROUND US

Movement and energy

- how do things work?

Change over Time

- how do things change?

Progression in WAU

- identify similarities and differences between living things, places, objects and materials
- understand that different materials behave in different ways, have different properties and can be used for different purposes
- understand that materials can be joined/assembled in different ways
- understand and use positional and directional language, as well as simple maps and drawings

PHYSICAL DEVELOPMENT AND MOVEMENT

- play/create/modify simple games
- listen and respond to a range of stimuli

Progression in PDM

- move with control and co-ordination
- move with confidence, imagination and safety
- use a range of small and large equipment appropriately
- handle small tools, objects, construction and malleable materials safely and with increasing control

LINKS TO THE FOUNDATION STAGE IN WALES

'Children learn through first hand experiential activities with the serious business of 'play' providing the vehicle. Through their play, children practise and consolidate their learning, play with ideas, experiment, take risks, solve problems, and make decisions individually, in small and large groups.'

Framework for Children's Learning for 3 to 7-year-olds in Wales

There are 7 Areas of Learning in the Foundation Phase:

Personal and Social Development, Well-Being and Cultural Diversity

Language, Literacy and Communication Skills

Mathematical Development

Welsh Language Development

Knowledge and Understanding of the World

Physical Development

Creative Development

Through using the planned Problem Solving activities in this book, development of the following skills will be supported. Other areas will also be developed, but less directly.

LANGUAGE, LITERACY AND COMMUNICATION SKILLS

- communicate by:
  – experiment with mark-making, using a variety of media
  – producing pieces of emergent writing
- communicate by using symbols, pictures and words
- follow stories read to them and respond as appropriate

MATHEMATICAL DEVELOPMENT

- select and use appropriate mathematical ideas, equipment and materials to solve practical problems
- develop a variety of mathematical approaches and strategies
- develop their mathematical language across the range of mathematics, and use it
- in their role play and in communicating/talking to adults about their work

KNOWLEDGE AND UNDERSTANDING OF THE WORLD

- exploring and experimenting
- identifying what they want to find out and how to do it
- thinking what might happen if…
- seeing links between cause and effect
- thinking creatively and imaginatively

PHYSICAL DEVELOPMENT

- develop fine manipulative skills
- use a range of small and large equipment and stimuli
- use and handle a range of tools
- understand rules and elements of games and be able to play simple cooperative and competitive games
- solve simple problems with a partner, such as how to find, retrieve or carry objects, score points etc
- use both large apparatus and small equipment
- begin to understand how important it is to lift, carry, place and use equipment safely

CREATIVE DEVELOPMENT

- explore and experiment with a variety of techniques and materials
- make choices when choosing materials and resources
- mix, shape, arrange and combine materials to create their own images and objects that communicate and express their ideas, feelings and memories creatively
- develop their understanding of planning, designing, modelling, modifying and reflecting
- use a variety of materials and tools for experimentation and Problem Solving
- design and make simple products and mechanisms
- explore a range of sound sources and experiment with different ways of making and organising sounds
- create their own musical ideas and contribute to simple compositions
- explore and express a range of moods and feelings through a variety of movements

THE ENVIRONMENT FOR PROBLEM SOLVING

The ethos of the setting is a vital element in developing a Problem Solving culture, and a number of factors need to be considered if you want to make Problem Solving a worthwhile part of the curriculum for both children and practitioners. You may wish to reflect on the practice in your setting and ask yourselves the following questions.

How do practitioners behave?

- Do they have a shared ethos regarding Problem Solving?
- Do they work together to promote Problem Solving opportunities, approaches and strategies?
- Do they support and scaffold children's learning through the use of skilled questioning?
- Are they aware that showing the children the solution without any understanding of the process is not going to develop their learning?
- Do they value process over product?
- Are they aware of the individual needs of the children so they are sensitive to those who need time to think or immediate support?
- Are they aware of strategies which they can use to support children to overcome frustration and disappointment?
- Is there a commitment to Problem Solving in written policy?

What are the expectations of the children?

- Are they given responsibility for decision making?
- Are they given opportunities to select from a wide range of areas, tools and materials?
- Are they given time and space to re-visit or re-create problems?
- Do they happily seek the assistance of an adult, confident in the knowledge that they will be supported and praised for their efforts?

What about the parents?

- Do they know about Problem Solving?
- Are they helped and encouraged to support this philosophy at home?

TEN TIPS FOR CREATING A PROBLEM SOLVING ENVIRONMENT

1. **Have a go!** Start small, try one day at a time. Take a few risks, build a few experiments into your planning.
2. **Make it natural:** Build thinking and Problem Solving into everything you do - let your natural creativity and the creativity of children emerge in the way you work together. Support collaboration, not competition. Remember Problem Solving isn't just about maths.
3. **Be with them:** Spend time with children as they are working. Model being a thinker yourself, and lead their thinking on by the way you talk, observe and question.
4. **Time:** Give time for thinking and Problem Solving, build it into your planning; give children time to think, to work things out and to talk.
5. **Talk:** Remember that language is at the heart of thinking, and children need language to think with.
6. **Questioning:** Encourage children to ask questions, pose problems and think about what they are doing. Practise asking open-ended questions yourself (open-ended questions invite more than one answer – it's not always easy!).
7. **Thinking everywhere:** Make both the indoors and the outdoor area places for thinking, not just physical activity.
8. **Resources:** Make sure resources are accessible, available and as open-ended as possible. Combine stability (resources in predictable places) with novelty (surprises and changes).
9. **Sustain the thinking:** Help children to think before they do something, during the activity and after they have finished.
10. **Involve everyone:** Children, parents, other staff, managers in thinking about thinking (this is called metacognition). If everyone is thinking, the children will get a consistent message about this vital skill for lifelong learning!

RESOURCES

Well-equipped settings will have a wealth of different resources to support Problem Solving approaches, but the ways in which these resources are made available and stored is almost more important than the resources themselves.

Resources should be organised so that access and selection is easy, even for the youngest of children. Children will get involved in solving problems wherever they are, but the resources they need should be carefully stored and presented in ways that make selection, use and return both easy and inviting.

- Store resources in containers labelled with a photograph and the name of the contents.
- Provide the widest range of different types and sizes of resources.
- Remind children frequently that if an item they require is not immediately available in the room, they can request it, and you will do your best to provide it.
- Use a photo inventory or catalogue for each area of the curriculum, and encourage children to look at and use it.

The following suggestions are just starters, and a further list with details of suppliers can be found in the Appendix section on pages 77.

Books/Literacy

a variety of story and poetry books which lend themselves to the addition of sounds or music; book making materials; mark making equipment of all sorts; white and clip-boards; lots of scrap paper

Construction

open-ended materials such as cardboard boxes, fabric, pegs, poles, rope, bulldog clips, tubes from carpet and fabric rolls, large elastic bands, single wheels and pairs with axles, lots of different glues, tapes and other fixing materials

Music/Sound Making

sound makers such as rainmaker, thunder tube, bicycle bell, animal sound tubs, boom whackers, squeakers, horns, bird calls; tape recorders; talking tins and materials to make their own sound makers

Outdoors

focus on open-ended materials such as camouflage nets, den building materials, fabric, scarves, clips and pegs; have a tap or large water container, a hose pipe, guttering and drainpipes, buckets and pulleys

Science/Investigation

a variety of plastic pipes and tubes including flexible ones, corner bends, joints, tape of all sorts, string, rope, a computer, cameras, tape recorders or dictaphones

ASKING QUESTIONS

One of the most important strategies in supporting children in Problem Solving is in the skillful use of questioning. Questions can help children to identify what the problem is and what they already know about it. They can help to simplify it by breaking it into steps and to create a plan.

Questioning should be supportive and scaffold the children's learning, but the practitioner should avoid filling in too many gaps or offering their own solutions. The questions posed should be open-ended, encouraging the child to:

- think
- plan
- predict
- explain
- recall
- describe
- compare
- re-tell
- ask questions and voice their own ideas and suggestions

thus essentially promoting the development of their language and thinking skills. Listen carefully to their answers, as these will show what they have noticed and what they consider important.

Open-ended questions have many possible answers, and often begin with What? How? or Why?

- What do you want to happen?
- What do you want it to do?
- What will happen if...?
- What could you do first/next/then/after that?
- How can you...?
- How could we...?
- Why are you...?
- Why do you think...?

However, be careful not to over-use questioning. In some instances, giving prompts or thinking aloud can be more supportive, as can your gesture and facial expression.

- I've seen something like this before.
- I remember whe...
- Can we find another way to...?
- I think I'll try ...
- I wonder if...?

Questioning can also be used at the end of the Problem Solving activity, giving the children the opportunity to review their work and discuss other options for another time.

EFFECTIVE PLANNING FOR PROBLEM SOLVING

Children need to practice the skills of Problem Solving in the company of adults (sustaining shared thinking). They also need to have Problem Solving skills explained, demonstrated and modelled by adults and other children, and to meet this need, you will be planning Problem Solving activities in all sorts of situations.

Some of these activities will be planned for adult led or adult directed sessions, where children can see the Problem Solving process in action. Planned, adult-directed Problem Solving activities can be incorporated into all areas in the setting and may be presented in a variety of ways to stimulate interest and curiosity. Combine these with more informally arranged discussions during periods of child-initiated learning. This combination might include:

- planning some of your regular adult directed sessions to include Problem Solving activities or elements;
- using different places the setting for planned group discussion activities – outside, in the role play area, in the construction, by the water tray, in a tent or shelter;
- sitting on a special square of carpet, carpet samples, cushions;
- encouraging children to suggest a discussion when they need it, not just when the programme says 'group time';
- calling children together informally to discuss problems as soon as they arise;
- having a special 'Problem Solving' sign - such as a rain stick, a flag or a musical instrument that means 'we need to talk', so you can pause in the busy day to discuss something that has just come up.

Of course, everyone needs to be aware of the impact of these activities on the time children have to play uninterrupted. Don't be tempted to use them too often, or they will lose their interest and just become a nuisance! Problem Solving will engage children for lengthy periods of time, so staff should take this into account when offering these activities, and should offer them at times when there are fewest interruptions.

In common with other areas of the Curriculum, there will be children who need additional support. Some children will come from backgrounds with little or no experiences of Problem Solving, others will be younger or with less well developed talking and thinking skills. Both will require thoughtful input by practitioners. Older, more able, or more experienced children may be ready for further challenges. By working independently or with minimal adult input, they may revisit an activity and continue to explore the resources, materials and tools to solve the problem in a new way, or to solve a new problem.

ENCOURAGING PROBLEM SOLVING SKILLS IN EVERYDAY ACTIVITIES

How can you ensure that Problem Solving becomes embedded in the ethos of your setting?

Take every opportunity to encourage the children to think and talk in a variety of situations, particularly those which arise regularly in the everyday life of the setting. Give examples and challenges that relate to the needs, interests and real-life situations and happenings, which are the most meaningful to the children.

These might include some of the following:

- The pens, pencils and scissors keep getting mixed up. How should we store them?
- If all the children want to play in the water (or sand, Lego, bricks) at the same time, what should we do?
- What should the rules be for the computer? sand? home corner?
- Some children want to play with the remote control car, (or computer, karaoke machine, new bike) for a long time. How can we make sure that everyone gets the same amount of time?
- Some children don't like sharing (or helping to tidy up, or sharing fairly). What should we do?
- Bits of games, jigsaws and toys keep getting lost. What do you think we could do?
- If someone had a toy that you wanted, what could you do?
- In the story we've just heard about ... what do you think about ...?

INVOLVING CHILDREN IN PLANNING

Involving children in planning also encourages their Problem Solving, thinking and talking skills. Some resources to support this can be found in the Appendix section on pages 75. Here are some starter ideas:

- What would you like to learn about?
- What do you know about...?
- Where would be the best place for...?
- Where could we go for an outing on a sunny day? or a snowy or rainy day?
- What other equipment or substances could we add to the water, construction, outdoor play?
- What can we change the role play area into next?
- Which resources will we need for...?
- What do you think was best about our last plan and why?

BUILDING PROBLEM SOLVING INTO YOUR CONTINUOUS PROVISION

Offering children problems to solve as they work in free choice activities is one way to embed Problem Solving into the culture of your setting. Try some of these:

- Leave familiar objects in unusual places to stimulate questions and hypotheses, such as a puppet in a tree, a toy down a hole, something outside the fence. Ask children to help find a solution to the problem
- Leave simple new resources such as a piece of guttering, a rope, a basket, a new piece of fabric, some clothes pegs, CDs to paint on, and see how children incorporate them in their play
- Put a ring in a box, a lost toy, a pair of big shoes in the play area so children are challenged to think about what they are, how they came to be there and how to get them back to their owner
- Remove a piece of essential or popular equipment, such as the ladder from the slide, and see whether the children can manage without it, by devising an alternative
- Try a day with no paintbrushes for the paint, bats but no balls, fruit but no knife to cut it, and let the children suggest what you could use instead
- Leave problems on cards for older children to read - make this an optional choice for them in the bricks, construction, sand etc

- Leave a note or message for children to find indoors or outside, explaining a problem that they could solve, such as someone who hasn't had any birthday cards, a lost pet needing a poster for the notice board, the secretary needing help with a job, a broken toy that needs fixing, a small object lost in the sand
- Build Problem Solving into every day by inviting children to solve simple problems and challenges such as a new way to serve snack, a different place to have the role play area, a way to help someone with no-one to play with, a different way to make a picture or tell a story.

MAKING OPPORTUNITIES TO PRACTISE PROBLEM SOLVING

Get into the habit of asking questions, posing problems, inviting alternatives in every aspect of your work with the children. Here are some examples:

In stories, pause and ask a simple question for discussion in pairs or as a group:

- What do you think will happen next?
- What should Eddie do now?
- Where are the children going?
- What do you need to go on a bear hunt?
- How could the story end a different way?
- What would you do if you were this character?
- Who could help them?
- What happened after the end of the story (or before the story starts)?
- Where would you hide it?

Out of doors, pose simple questions, problems and points to ponder:

- When do you think it will stop raining?
- How can we keep the shed tidy?
- Which toys shall we have out today?
- Where do you think that plane is going?
- What do you think your mum/dad is doing now?
- What do you think is for snack today?
- What is above the clouds?
- How do plants grow?
- How could you teach someone to skip?
- How do baby birds get out of their shells?

As you work alongside them, reflect on the things you are using and doing:

- How does the glue get in a glue-stick?
- How do pencils (or paper clips) get made?
- What is paper made from?
- How could two children paint at one easel?
- How could we make an envelope?
- What would we do if there were no paintbrushes?
- How can we make sure the tops go back on the felt pens?
- Could you make a boat from paper?
- How do scissors work?

and **during group time** or when you are just chatting, try some 'What if...' ideas:

- What if children were the teachers and teachers were the children?
- What if all felt pens were pink?
- What if dogs could fly?
- What if we wore swimming costumes in the winter?
- What if dinosaurs were alive now?

Just let your imagination flow, keep thinking, questioning, talking and sharing ideas.

BUILDING PROBLEM SOLVING INTO YOUR PLANNED ACTIVITIES FOR GROUPS AND INDIVIDUALS

Plan to include small problems to solve in adult-initiated or adult-directed activities, so Problem Solving is not just about numeracy, but about thinking in every area of learning. Try some of these:

- Give plenty of time for children to think together about what a new word says;
- At the beginning of a topic or theme, ask the children how you could find out more about minibeasts, the seaside, dinosaurs or whatever your focus is;
- Challenge children to collect the things they will need for an activity you are doing together, make the preparation part of the activity;
- After you have introduced an activity, ask the children how they would like to do it - we are going to make Mothers' Day cards. How would you like to do it? What would you like to use? What will you need?
- Sometimes ask the children where they would like the activity to happen - even if it is adult directed. The home corner, outside, the book area, in a tent are all places children like to be, so ask them how you could manage to do the activity in the place they have chosen and whether there will be any problems or difficulties;
- Plan the beginning of the activity and then ask the children what needs to be done next. Follow their ideas and meet the challenges and solve any problems that may arise. This may feel risky for you, but it's very good for thinking skills!
- Pause to use Problem Solving techniques in stories as you tell them. Ask children what they think a character could do, what may happen next, how to solve a problem. Make up stories and let them go with children's ideas - you just need to start them off, and children love them;
- Give children opportunities to use new equipment or familiar equipment in new places and ways.

PLANNED PROBLEM SOLVING ACTIVITIES

Sometimes you will want to focus more directly on Problem Solving skills, so children have time to learn the skills and practice the techniques they need. It also gives you an opportunity to model being a Problem Solving adult.

Problem Solving sessions should be planned at times when you can really concentrate on one thing, and shape children's learning by supporting their thinking and offering real problems to solve. These problems work best if they are relevant to children's interests and are flexible, so you can respond to the pace, concentration and maturity of the group you are working with.

Remember, Problem Solving and challenges don't have to be about things going wrong!

Try some real problems like these:

- How can we stop the rain coming in through the door during outside time when we leave the doors open?
- The bikes take up a lot of space, and they get in the way of the children who want to play football. What can we do about this problem?
- Yesterday we had to do lots of puzzles, because they all fell off the shelf. How can we arrange the puzzles so they don't fall off again?
- I've just had a letter from the lady who lives next door to our school. She says that some children are climbing on her fence and breaking it. What can we do?
- We are going on a trip next week and we haven't got enough grown-ups to keep us all safe. What can we do?
- This camera/tape recorder/CD player is new and the instructions weren't in the box. What should we do?
- All the footballs are on the roof. How can we get them down?
- It's going to be very sunny today. How could we make some shady places to play and sit?
- I collected all these conkers/stones/leaves/seeds at the weekend. What could we do with them?
- Some of the boys love playing superheroes, but they make a lot of noise and some of the children get scared. What should we do?

INVOLVING PARENTS AND CARERS IN PROBLEM SOLVING

Many parents are keen to support your work at home, and through carefully planned liaison, you can work together to foster links in children's learning.

Newsletters, leaflets, home learning link sheets, handouts, Parents' Meetings and workshops are some of the ways you could try. And here are some suggestions for simple things parents can do to help their child develop Problem Solving, thinking and talking skills at home:

Encourage practical activities such as:

- baking, gardening, DIY projects, decorating, mending things
- making sandwiches or toast
- pairing socks and shoes
- sharing out cake, fruit or other food
- helping to pack groceries away
- setting the table
- tidying away toys.

It is particularly helpful to children if you spend a little time with them at the end of the day or at bedtime. Remembering what has happened just before they go to sleep really helps memory.

Play memory games such as:

- 'Granny went to market and bought...'
- 'When we went to the zoo we saw...'
- 'Pairs' using cards or pictures from magazines
- 'Kim's Game' (spotting what has been removed from a small selection of objects)
- 'I Spy'.

Support thinking skills by:

- encouraging the child to help plan a trip, a party, a meal
- encouraging them to choose appropriate clothes to wear
- involving them in making simple family rules
- using open-ended questions.

Extend their language skills by:

- giving them access to a wide range of experiences such as outings, picnics, museum visits, shopping trips, sports, theatre, cinema, pantomime, fairs and fetes, parks and open spaces
- talking with them and listening to what they have to say.

Part 2
PLANNED PROBLEM SOLVING ACTIVITIES

Planned Problem Solving Activities

The following pages contain a range of planned Problem Solving challenges for children, linked to areas and aspects of the Early Years curriculum. These are intended to give you ideas of the sorts of starters you could offer to children in your group. They are not intended to be used exclusively, or to form a 'programme', they are just examples. Some aspects may seem repetitive e.g. Ideas for Presentation; page number referrals, but these activities are 'stand-alone' and not progressive. The selection can be dipped into. You will think of many more and many will arise naturally as you become more familiar with the process and more confident with the activity. The challenges you invent yourselves will be more relevant to the setting and the children you work with.

Close observation and/or interaction during the activities and reflection afterwards will enable you to monitor and record each child's development and learning. Next steps in planning can then be identified, incorporating additional support or challenge to provide for each child's current needs.

Each of the planned activities can be introduced by letter, card or recorded on a 'Talking' resource (see page 75 for suggestions and suppliers).

Creating a Problem Solving Bank may involve you:

- setting up a folder or file for Problem Solving containing resources, and support material and information for practitioners
- making cards or letters for each of the activities
- colour coding the activities in accordance with the curriculum links for easy access
- recording cards and letters onto your chosen ICT resources and adding them to the bank
- storing resource materials in clearly labelled bags or boxes
- including a planning/recording grid

Examples of a Problem Solving card, a letter and a planning/recording grid can be found on pages 78–80.

It is only through experimentation and practice that children truly learn what we as adults are aiming to teach them.

Make a bag

Can you make a bag?

WHAT YOU NEED

In addition to the available resources:

- a 'tool box' containing a variety of tape, glue, staplers, string, scissors, hole punches etc

IDEAS FOR PRESENTATION

- use the template from the Problem Solving bank to make a card
- record on one of the 'Talking' resources (see p75)

USEFUL VOCABULARY

- handle
- flap
- fastening
- clip
- straps
- shoulder
- handbag
- clutch bag

WHAT YOU DO

1. Using one of the suggested stimuli, present the problem to the children and discuss.
2. Talk about different types of bags for different purposes.
3. Allow them to decide whether to work alone or in pairs.
4. Give them time to select the resources they need.
5. As they work, support their attempts using scaffolding and open-ended questions (see p14) to encourage their thinking and talking skills.
6. Let them show their efforts to each other.

TAKING IT FURTHER

- Photograph the process.
- Make different kinds of bags e.g. a rucksack; for the postman; for shopping; for school.

AND ANOTHER THING...

Ask the children what kind of bag they would need to move lots of brick; carry an animal; put a French loaf in; carry water

LINKS TO EARLY LEARNING GOALS

EA&D 1 Exploring and using media and materials
EA&D 2 Being imaginative
PD 1 Moving and handling

A Small World castle

Can you make a castle for the Small World people?

WHAT YOU NEED

In addition to the available resources:

- small flags
- pictures of castles
- a 'tool box' containing scissors, glue, string, staplers, a variety of tape etc

WHAT YOU DO

1. Using one of the suggested stimuli, present the problem to the children and discuss.
2. Look at the pictures of castles and talk about what makes them different from our houses.
3. Allow them to decide whether to work alone, in pairs or in groups.
4. Give them time to select the resources they need.
5. As they work, support their attempts using scaffolding and open-ended questions (see p14), to encourage their thinking and talking skills.
6. Let them show their efforts to each other.

TAKING IT FURTHER

- Photograph the process.
- Make a drawing or a plan.
- Make different structures for the Small World people e.g. vehicles, houses.

AND ANOTHER THING...

Look at books of homes and buildings, past and present.

Discuss what it might be like to live in a cave, a wooden hut, a tent or a treehouse and what problems there might be.

USEFUL VOCABULARY

- castle
- turret
- ramparts
- drawbridge
- flagpole
- gate

IDEAS FOR PRESENTATION

- use the template from the Problem Solving bank to make a card
- record on one of the 'Talking' resources (see p75)
- use the template from the Problem Solving bank to write a letter from one of the Small World people

LINKS TO EARLY LEARNING GOALS

EA&D 1 Exploring and using media and materials
EA&D 2 Being imaginative
PD 1 Moving and handling

Scary Mask!

Can you make a scary mask to frighten everyone?

WHAT YOU NEED

In addition to choice from the general resources:

- a 'tool box' containing elastic bands, string, hole punches, ring reinforcements etc

USEFUL VOCABULARY

- frighten
- scare
- dangerous
- dark
- jaggy
- spiky
- googly
- hairy
- fierce
- fangs
- teeth
- sharp
- pointed
- shape

WHAT YOU DO

1. Present the problem to the group of children using one of the suggested stimuli and discuss.
2. Talk about different kinds of masks and how they stay on your face.
3. Allow the children to select their required resources from the art and design area and the 'tool box'.
4. Support their efforts using scaffolding and open-ended questions (see p14) to encourage thinking and talking skills.
5. Discuss and help them in their attempts with cutting out eyes, fastenings etc. if they want it, making sure that you do not solve the problem directly for them.
6. Finally, encourage them to talk about their masks and what makes them scary.

TAKING IT FURTHER

- Design or draw the mask before starting to make it.
- Photograph the finished mask or the stages of making it.

Then you could:

- Make a friendly/sad/happy/surprised or angry mask.
- Make animal masks of jungle animals, imaginary animals or pets.

AND ANOTHER THING...

Use masks to talk about feelings and expressions.

'How could we make a play that uses all our masks?'

'Who wears a mask in their job?'

IDEAS FOR PRESENTATION

- use the template from the Problem Solving bank to write a letter from a child going to a fancy dress party
- record on one of the 'Talking' resources (see p75)

LINKS TO EARLY LEARNING GOALS

EA&D 1 Exploring and using media and materials

EA&D 2 Being imaginative

PD 1 Moving and handling

Bear Hunt

Can you add sounds to the story 'We're all Going on a Bear Hunt?

WHAT YOU NEED

In addition to choice from the general resources:

- the book 'We're all Going on a Bear Hunt' – Michael Rosen and Helen Oxenbury
- flannel, small world or magnetic pictures of the story
- a selection of sound makers

WHAT YOU DO

1. Present the problem to the group of children using one of the suggested stimuli, and discuss what they think they could do.
2. Revisit the story using story board, small world people and animals, or magnetic pictures on a board.
3. Discuss the words and sounds in the story and what might be used to represent them.
4. Encourage the children to select sound makers and talk about when and how they could be used.
5. Re-read the story, with the children experimenting with their sounds.
6. Support their attempts by using scaffolding and open-ended questions (see p14) to encourage their thinking and talking skills.
7. Discuss their work and thinking, making sure that you do not solve the problem for them.
8. Re-read the story with the sound effects.

IDEAS FOR PRESENTATION

- use the template from the Problem Solving bank to make a card
- record on one of the 'Talking' resources (see p75)

USEFUL VOCABULARY

In addition to choice from the general resources:

- bear
- children
- grass
- swishy
- swashy
- river
- splash
- splosh
- mud
- squelch
- squerch
- forest
- snowstorm
- stumble
- trip
- hoo
- woo
- cave
- tiptoe
- googly

TAKING IT FURTHER

- Record the story with the sounds.
- Try different sound makers.
- Help the children to make a story bag or sack with all the things they would need to re-play the story.

Then you could:

- Add sounds to other stories.
- Add sounds to rhymes and poems.
- Make up your own stories with sounds.

AND ANOTHER THING...

Make music out of doors, telling the story in movement and music.

'How do instruments work?'

LINKS TO EARLY LEARNING GOALS

C&L	1	Listening and attention
EA&D	2	Being imaginative
PD	1	Moving and handling

Animal Rhyme

Can you make up a poem or rhyme for an animal?

WHAT YOU NEED

In addition to the available resources:

- a selection of puppets or Small World animals

WHAT YOU DO

1. Using one of the suggested stimuli, present the problem to the children and discuss.
2. Talk about other poems and rhymes about animals they already know.
3. Allow them to decide whether to work alone or in pairs.
4. Support their attempts using scaffolding and open-ended questions (see p14).
5. Let them recite their poems or rhymes to the other children.

TAKING IT FURTHER

- Record the poems and rhymes.
- Draw or paint the picture of the poem or rhyme.
- Use different toys e.g. people, sea creatures, vehicles.

Then you could:

- Make a friendly/sad/happy/surprised or angry mask.
- Make animal masks of jungle animals, imaginary animals or pets.

AND ANOTHER THING...

- Play rhyming games
- Play alliteration games

USEFUL VOCABULARY

- poem
- rhyme
- words
- sounds
- funny
- sad
- angry

IDEAS FOR PRESENTATION

- use the template from the Problem Solving bank to make a card
- record on one of the 'Talking' resources (see p75)

LINKS TO EARLY LEARNING GOALS

L	1	Reading
EA&D	2	Being imaginative
C&L	1	Listening and attention

Funny Story

The little boy is sad. Can you make up a funny story to make him laugh?

WHAT YOU NEED

In addition to choice from the general resources:

- a picture of a sad boy

USEFUL VOCABULARY

In addition to choice from the general resources:

- sad
- unhappy
- story
- funny
- feelings
- laugh
- giggle
- happy
- cry
- title
- beginning
- middle
- ending

WHAT YOU DO

1. Present the problem to the group of children using one of the suggested stimuli and discuss how they might help.
2. Talk about what they think is funny and makes them laugh.
3. Let the children choose to work independently or in pairs to create a funny story.
4. Allow them to select any resources they require such as puppets, pictures, clothing, masks or sound-makers.
5. Support their thinking, using scaffolding and open-ended questions (see p14) to encourage their thinking and talking skills.
6. Work with them if they want it, ensuring that you do not solve the problem for them.
7. Finally, give some time to listening to each other's stories and commenting on them.

TAKING IT FURTHER

- Record the stories.
- Draw the stories.
- Make a book about the story.

Then you could:

- Make up a sad/scary/exciting or fairy story.
- Make up a funny/scary or exciting poem or rhyme.

IDEAS FOR PRESENTATION

- use the template from the Problem Solving bank to write a letter from a little boy
- an e-mail
- use the template from the Problem Solving bank to make a card
- record on one of the 'Talking' resources (see p75)

AND ANOTHER THING...

Go outside and tell or act out the funny stories – take some photos of the children telling the stories and listening to others.

Ask *'What makes people laugh?'*

LINKS TO EARLY LEARNING GOALS

C&L ❸ Speaking

EA&D ❷ Being imaginative

Giraffe House

The giraffe doesn't like getting wet when it rains. Can you make a house for him?

In addition to choice from the general resources:

- a selection of toy or small world giraffes

USEFUL VOCABULARY

• giraffe	• tall	• body	• neck
• rain	• wet	• house	• walls
• high	• bricks	• blocks	• roof
• door	• window	• sides	• strong

WHAT YOU DO

1. Present the problem to the group of children using one of the suggested stimuli, and discuss.
2. Talk about the shape and height of giraffes.
3. Let the children decide whether to work alone, in pairs or in groups.
4. Help them to choose one of the giraffes and some of the resources in the construction area.
5. Support their work by using scaffolding and open-ended questions (see p14) to encourage thinking and talking skills.
6. Discuss and support their progress, without solving the problem for them.
7. Finally, let everyone look at each giraffe house and share comments about the process and the finished shelters.

TAKING IT FURTHER

- Design or draw the house before starting the construction.
- Photograph the process or the end product.
- Test the shelters to see if they are really waterproof.

Then you could:

- Build or make houses for other animals.
- Build or make houses for people.
- Build or make enclosures and other structures, experimenting with waterproof materials and joining methods.

AND ANOTHER THING...

Work in the art and design area to test and experiment with materials and structures, including the use of wood, plastic and other resistant materials.

'Can you make a shelter outside that is big enough for children to use?'

IDEAS FOR PRESENTATION

- use the template from the Problem Solving bank to write a letter from the giraffe (or a photo)
- use the template from the Problem Solving bank to make a card
- record on one of the 'Talking' resources (see p75)

LINKS TO EARLY LEARNING GOALS

EA&D	1	Exploring and using media and materials
PD	1	Moving and handling
M	2	Shape, space and measures
EA&D	2	Being imaginative

Boat Building

Can you build or make a boat with a sail, that is big enough for two children?

WHAT YOU NEED

In addition to choice from the general resources:

- a selection of fabric
- flags
- flagpoles or sticks
- oars or resources to represent them

WHAT YOU DO

1. Using one of the suggested stimuli, talk about the problem with the children, listening to their suggestions and solutions to the problem or challenge.
2. Talk about the best things to use for a big construction and what else they need.
3. Let the children decide whether to work alone, in pairs or as a group, and give them time to select from the resources in the construction area or recycled materials.
4. Stay near so you can support their work as they build. This scale of construction is complex and may need some help, but don't offer it until they ask!
5. Give plenty of time for them to experiment and play in the boats they have constructed.

LINKS TO EARLY LEARNING GOALS

EA&D 1 Exploring and using media and materials
PD 1 Moving and handling
M 2 Shape, space and measures
EA&D 2 Being imaginative

USEFUL VOCABULARY

- size
- base
- sides
- shape
- bow
- stern
- mast
- attach
- sail
- rope
- support
- stand
- hoist
- oars
- flag
- flagpole
- seats

IDEAS FOR PRESENTATION

- use the template from the Problem Solving bank to write a letter or problem card
- record on one of the 'Talking' resources (see p75)

TAKING IT FURTHER

- Design or draw the boat before starting to build it.
- Photograph the process and the finished boats.

Then you could:

- Introduce further activities using large or open-ended materials for construction, for example:
  – build or make an aeroplane to hold four children
  – build or make a train to hold five children
  – build or make a bus to hold lots of children
  – build or make a space rocket to hold three children.

AND ANOTHER THING...

Offer children a variety of construction, den-making and physical resources including natural materials.

'We need to protect our seeds from the birds. How could we do it?'

'Please make a sign to say it's cold outside and everyone needs to wear their coat.'

Buggy or Trolley?

Can you make a buggy or trolley that can move and carry one child?

WHAT YOU NEED

In addition to choice from the general resources:

- a wide selection of large scale construction materials and recycled objects such as tyres, wheels, planks, guttering etc.
- a selection of horns, hooters or bells

WHAT YOU DO

1. Present the problem to the group of children using one of the suggested stimuli and discuss.
2. Discuss the scale of the construction required and look at wheels, planks, joining and fixing systems.
3. Let the children decide whether to work alone, in pairs or as a group.
4. Help them to select from the resources in the construction area.
5. Support their attempts using scaffolding and open-ended questions (see p14) to encourage thinking and talking skills.
6. Be available to discuss their progress and give assistance with fastenings etc. if required, but don't solve the problem for them.
7. Arrange a time when they can demonstrate their buggies, wheelbarrows, carts, prams and discuss how well they work.

USEFUL VOCABULARY

- base
- scare
- move
- roll
- turn
- slide
- wheels
- axle
- nut
- bolt
- pull
- push
- tow
- safe
- strong
- buggy
- cart
- wheelbarrow
- pram
- trolley

TAKING IT FURTHER

- Design or draw the buggy before they start.
- Photograph the process of making the buggies or the finished vehicles.

Then you could:

- Build, make or invent a buggy that can move a few children at a time.
- Make a vehicle for moving bricks, sand or boxes around the outdoor area.

AND ANOTHER THING...

Pose problems and challenges out of doors:

'How do pushchairs fold up?'

'Can girls play football?'

'Why don't birds fall out of the sky?'

'How many things can you find that will move down a slope?'

IDEAS FOR PRESENTATION

- use the template from the Problem Solving bank to make a card
- use the template from the Problem Solving bank to write a letter or card from a child in another group
- a phone call

LINKS TO EARLY LEARNING GOALS

EA&D	1	Exploring and using media and materials
PD	1	Moving and handling
M	2	Shape, space and measures
EA&D	2	Being imaginative

Construction

Glueless Person

Can you join some of these shapes to make a person, without using glue?

WHAT YOU NEED

In addition to choice from the general resources:

- a selection of pre-cut card shapes (e.g. circles, rectangles etc. of different sizes)
- a tool box containing a variety of tapes, hole punch, paper clips and fasteners, string etc.

WHAT YOU DO

1. Talk about the problem with the group of children using one of the suggested stimuli. Talk about alternative ways of fastening.
2. Talk about bodies and the position, shape and length of bodies, heads, arms and legs.
3. Explore the different shapes you have offered, and let the children select shapes and tools they want to work with.
4. Support using scaffolding and open-ended questions to encourage their thinking and talking skills.
5. Talk about their progress, and help with the use of the tools if they need it, ensuring that you do not solve the problem for them.
6. Finally, let them show their shape people to each other and share comments on the task.

TAKING IT FURTHER

- Design or draw the person before you start.
- Decorate it when it is finished, adding features, hair, clothes etc.
- Use paper fasteners to make moving parts.

USEFUL VOCABULARY

- circle • square • rectangle • triangle
- long • short • body • head • arm
- leg • position • length • attach
- tape • hole • punch • paper
- clip • string • paper • fastener
- treasury • tag

IDEAS FOR PRESENTATION

- use the template from the Problem Solving bank to make a card
- record on one of the 'Talking' resources (see p75)

Then you could:

- Make an animal, an alien, a bird using shapes.
- Give your figure a moving head, arms, legs and tail.
- Make a vehicle from shapes. Look at some pictures before you start, or do a drawing.
- Make some moving parts in your model.

AND ANOTHER THING...

Use your construction area to make models with moving parts.

'Can you make a car with moving wheels?'

'How does a clock work?'

'Can you make a model from wood without using nails?'

LINKS TO EARLY LEARNING GOALS

M	2	Shape, space and measures
EA&D	1	Exploring and using media and materials
EA&D	2	Being imaginative
PD	1	Moving and handling

What a Mix-up!

The toys and games in the cupboard are all mixed up. Can you help to sort them out?

WHAT YOU NEED

In addition to choice from the general resources:

- a large tray – containing a variety of 'mixed-up' table games
- original or new boxes
- labels and mark makers

WHAT YOU DO

1. Set out the tray of 'mixed up' resources and the original or new boxes.
2. Present the problem to the children using one of the suggested stimuli and discuss how they could solve the challenge.
3. Let them decide whether to work alone, in pairs or as a group.
4. Support their attempts using scaffolding or open-ended questions to encourage their Problem Solving skills.
5. Keep in touch by visiting the activity, and discuss their progress – don't solve the problem for them.
6. Look at the completed games and if they do not have an original box ask the children to suggest names for labelling the new ones and share comments.

IDEAS FOR PRESENTATION

- use the template from the Problem Solving bank to write a letter from someone in the setting (maybe your manager!)
- use the template from the Problem Solving bank to make a card
- record on one of the 'Talking' resources (see p75)

USEFUL VOCABULARY

- same
- different
- material
- wood
- plastic
- paper
- shape
- colour
- size
- board
- game
- toy
- jigsaw
- piece
- counter
- same
- different
- sort
- group

TAKING IT FURTHER

- Include more pieces.
- Add some odd items that don't fit any of the games.

Then you could:

- Use the same process for reorganising outdoor equipment, lost property boxes etc.
- Children love organising things, let them suggest ways of organising mark-making equipment, outdoor play things, recycled materials for construction etc.

AND ANOTHER THING...

Get children involved in reorganising your room or making the space or resources more accessible.

'The drawer in my desk is very untidy, can you suggest a way of sorting it out?'

'Where should we put this new toy, so everyone can find it?'

'The book corner gets very untidy, how can we keep it tidy?'

LINKS TO EARLY LEARNING GOALS

PD	1	Moving and handling
UW	2	The world
M	2	Shape, space and measure

A Piece of Cake

A girl is having a birthday party and is inviting three friends. Can you divide the birthday cake so that everyones gets a piece of equal size?

WHAT YOU NEED

In addition to choice from the general resources:

- playdough and cutters
- candles
- pictures of birthday cakes

USEFUL VOCABULARY

- cake
- birthday
- round
- circle
- rectangle
- square
- triangle
- divide
- cut
- slice
- knife
- cutter
- same
- equal
- three
- four
- share
- whole
- half
- quarter

WHAT YOU DO

1. Present the problem to the children using one of the suggested starting points and discuss.
2. Talk about birthdays and cutting cakes.
3. Encourage the children to select the resources they need to make the cakes and solve the problem.
4. Support them, using scaffolding and open-ended questions (see p14) and encouraging thinking and talking skills.
5. Talk with them as they work, ensuring that you do not get in the way of their thinking or solve the problem for them.
6. Finally, share the solutions to the problem, and ask the children what they think is the best way to divide the birthday cake out fairly.

TAKING IT FURTHER

- Photograph the processes or record what the children are saying as they work.
- Draw the solutions – in one or a series of pictures.
- Make or buy a real cake and divide it up among all the children.

Then you could:

- Divide cakes among more children.
- Share out sweets or fruit.
- Find a way to share out a jug of liquid such as milk, juice or water.

AND ANOTHER THING...

Set some Problem Solving challenges in your Home Corner.

'Can you cut this apple into five pieces?'

'How could we make the home corner into a Pet Shop?'

'If we wanted to have a Home Corner outside, what would we need?'

IDEAS FOR PRESENTATION

- use the template from the Problem Solving bank to write a letter or invitation from a child
- use the template from the Problem Solving bank to make a card
- record on one of the 'Talking' resources (see p75)

LINKS TO EARLY LEARNING GOALS

M 1 Numbers

M 2 Shape, space and measures

PD 1 Moving and handling

Happy Music

Can you invent some happy music for the other children to dance to?

WHAT YOU NEED

In addition to choice from the general resources:

- pictures of dancers
- pictures of bands and orchestras
- simple musical instruments

USEFUL VOCABULARY

- happy
- fast
- jumpy
- bouncy
- jerky
- spiky
- loud
- spin
- twirl
- hop
- clap
- partner
- space
- jingle
- ring
- beat
- rhythm
- shake
- bang
- rattle

WHAT YOU DO

1. Present the problem to the group of children using one of the suggested stimuli, and discuss.
2. Talk about bands and what kind of instruments, rhythms, sounds make them feel happy.
3. Let them choose whether to work alone, in pairs or in groups.
4. Allow the children time for free play and exploration before using the instruments or sound makers for the problem.
5. Scaffold their thinking, by sensitive comments and open-ended questions (see p14). Don't be tempted to take over, or influence their decisions and solutions.
6. Let them take turns to play their music for the other children to dance to.

IDEAS FOR PRESENTATION

- use the template from the Problem Solving bank to write a letter from some children in another group
- record a message on one of the 'Talking' resources (see p75)

TAKING IT FURTHER

- Record the music.

Then you could:

- Repeat the activity to produce music for dances of different moods such as:
  - sad
  - slow
  - floaty
  - angry.
- Put on a show of dance and music.
- Make your own instruments.

AND ANOTHER THING...

Outdoors –

'How could we make some wind chimes for our garden?'

'Can you use these old saucepans to make a musical instrument?'

'Could you make a musical instrument for calling birds?'

'How many different sorts of sounds can you hear outside? How could you record them?'

LINKS TO EARLY LEARNING GOALS

EA&D ❶ Exploring and using media and materials
EA&D ❷ Being imaginative
PD ❶ Moving and handling

Scary Sounds

Can you add scary sounds to the poem 'In the Dark, Dark Wood'?

WHAT YOU NEED

In addition to choice from the general resources:

- a picture of the poem (or the book of the story) – see resources p76
- the poem on a tape

USEFUL VOCABULARY

- scary • wood • cottage • room
- cupboard • shelf • box • eerie • creepy
- dark • night • moon • shadow • creak
- squeak • groan • scream • fright
- monster • ghost • skeleton

WHAT YOU DO

1. Introduce the problem to the group of children using one of the suggested stimuli and discuss what they might need.
2. Talk about the picture, read the book or say the poem together.
3. Let the children decide whether to work alone, in pairs or in groups.
4. Allow the children plenty of time for free play and exploration before selecting which instruments they will use.
5. Support them by scaffolding their thinking and asking open-ended questions.
6. Talk about what is happening, but don't interfere unless they ask for help, and don't do it for them!
7. When everyone is ready, take turns at performing the music while the others say the poem.

IDEAS FOR PRESENTATION

- a greetings card with a relevant picture and the message inside
- record on one of the 'Talking' resources (see p75)
- a request from an adult for a sound track for a play or story

TAKING IT FURTHER

- Record the different versions with the words as well.

Then you could:

- Repeat the activity using poems of different genres or moods or recordings of stories and poetry.
- Make your own instruments from found materials to accompany stories, rhymes and poems.

AND ANOTHER THING...

Outdoors –

'How could we use these old knives, forks and spoons to make a musical mobile outside?'

'Can you use these plastic buckets to make music?'

'Here are some chiffon scarves. Can you make up a dance about the wind?'

LINKS TO EARLY LEARNING GOALS

EA&D ❶ Exploring and using media and materials

EA&D ❷ Being imaginative

Making Music

The band is late. Can you add music to a favourite song and fill in for them?

WHAT YOU NEED

In addition to choice from the general resources:

- props or photographs of song props to help the children to select
- CDs and books of words of favourite songs

WHAT YOU DO

1. Using the suggested stimuli, talk about the problem together, exploring favourite songs and music.
2. Look at the song props or pictures and select a song that everyone likes.
3. Repeat the challenge, discussing the type and mood of the song you have chosen.
4. Look at the instruments together and give the children time to select an instrument to play in the band.
5. Working as a group is difficult, be around to support negotiation and exploration of the music the band is producing. Don't do it for them – negotiation is part of Problem Solving.
6. Find an audience to listen to the song.

TAKING IT FURTHER

- Record the band playing their music.

Then you could:

- Try different instruments.
- Repeat using songs of different styles and moods.
- Accompany music on CD or the radio.
- Find a friend to be the singer for your group.

USEFUL VOCABULARY

- percussion • instrument • beat • rhythm
- time • happy • sad • lively • fast
- slow • introduction • ending • chorus

IDEAS FOR PRESENTATION

- use the template from the Problem Solving bank to write a letter from someone with the words of their favourite song
- use the template from the Problem Solving bank to make a card
- record on one of the 'Talking' resources (see p75)

AND ANOTHER THING...

Try karaoke and other technical supports for music making.

Here is a tape recorded story. Can you make a sound track?'

'Can you make some music to accompany this bubble machine?'

'What is a parade? How could we have one?'

'It's someone's birthday. Can we make up a birthday party song for them and record it?'

'The microphone is missing from the karaoke machine, Can you make a new one?'

LINKS TO EARLY LEARNING GOALS

EA&D ❶ Exploring and using media and materials

EA&D ❷ Being imaginative

PD ❶ Moving and handling

Hungry Crocodile

A big hungry crocodile lives in the river. Can you think of a way to get across without being eaten?

WHAT YOU NEED

In addition to choice from the general resources:

- a toy, puppet or small world crocodile
- blue fabric to represent the river

WHAT YOU DO

1. Introduce the problem to the children and discuss different ways of solving it.
2. Talk about different ways of crossing rivers.
3. Let the children decide whether to work alone, in pairs or in groups (this may be restricted by the number and variety of resources available).
4. If it isn't already in place, help the children to set up the fabric 'river', then select their resources.
5. Support their thinking, using open-ended questions (see p14) to encourage their thinking and talking skills. Stay with them, or visit frequently, ensuring that you do not solve the problem for them.
6. Try each of the other ideas and talk about how each one worked, and how the children solved the problem.

TAKING IT FURTHER

Design or draw the ideas before starting.

- Photograph the process and the solutions.

Then you could:

- Make the river wider.
- Try other ways to cross.
- Turn the work into a story and act it out with a crocodile character and children using different ways to get across.

USEFUL VOCABULARY

- river
- crocodile
- hungry
- eat
- safe
- cross
- step
- run
- jump
- leap
- bridge
- over
- span
- dam
- under
- support
- hold

IDEAS FOR PRESENTATION

- use the template from the Problem Solving bank to make a card
- a message left on the fabric river
- a recorded message

AND ANOTHER THING...

Help children to use Problem Solving techniques to address things that scare or worry them.

'How could you make a spell to stop spiders coming in your house?'

'What do you know about ghosts? Are they real?'

'Can toads really turn into princes?'

LINKS TO EARLY LEARNING GOALS

PD1 ❶ Moving and handling

EA&D ❷ Being imaginative

Obstacle Course

Can you get to the other side of the obstacle course without putting your feet onthe floor?

WHAT YOU NEED

In addition to the available resources:

- a selection of equipment suitable to form an obstacle course

WHAT YOU DO

1. Using one of the suggested stimuli, present the problem to the children and discuss.
2. Talk about other parts of their bodies they could use to travel, either by themselves or with a partner.
3. Allow them to decide whether to work alone or in pairs.
4. Support their attempts using scaffolding and open-ended questions (see p14) if they encounter an obstacle which is causing them difficulties.
5. Let them demonstrate their ideas for the other children to try out.

TAKING IT FURTHER

- Use different obstacles.
- Allow the children to choose the obstacles for the course.
- Cross the course allowing 1 foot to touch the ground; 1 hand and 1 foot; 2 hands and 1 foot.

IDEAS FOR PRESENTATION

- use the template from the Problem Solving bank to make a card
- record on one of the 'Talking' resources (see p75)

USEFUL VOCABULARY

- obstacle • slide • crawl • pull • push
- roll • tummy • knees • elbows • ankle
- side • wiggle • over • under • round
- between • across • carefully • safety

AND ANOTHER THING...

Use 'obstacles' for other physical activities – cones for cycling round; 'brick' walls for jumping over; cross bars for crawling/sliding under etc.

Discuss Health and Safety issues with the children regarding handling and using the equipment.

LINKS TO EARLY LEARNING GOALS

PD 1 Moving and handling

Fast Dance

Can you invent a fast dance using the music 'The Flight of the Bumblebee'?

WHAT YOU NEED

In addition to choice from the general resources:

- a tape or CD of the music – 'The Flight of the Bumble Bee' by Rimsky-Korsakov
- cassette, MP3 or CD player
- pictures of bees and flowers

IDEAS FOR PRESENTATION

- use the template from the Problem Solving bank to make a card
- record on one of the 'Talking' resources (see p75)
- an invitation from a bee!

WHAT YOU DO

1. Present the challenge to the children, listen to the music and look at the pictures or books you have collected.
2. Talk and think about the problem with the children, discussing different sounds and instruments.
3. Let the children decide whether to work alone, in pairs or in groups.
4. Support their attempts and encourage their thinking and talking skills as they discuss and work on solving the problem.
5. Discuss their efforts, ensuring that you do not solve the problem for them.
6. Have a session where everyone shows their music and dances to the rest of the children.

USEFUL VOCABULARY

- music
- composer
- orchestra
- instruments
- flight
- bumble bee
- flower
- pollen
- nectar
- start
- stop
- fast
- quick
- buzz
- run
- zig-zag
- ending

TAKING IT FURTHER

- Record the music and dances on video camera.
- Draw a picture of the dance.

Then you could:

- Show the dance or the video to other children or parents.
- Invent dances for slow, dreamy, angry, scary music.
- Invent dances for music from other countries or cultures.

AND ANOTHER THING...

Don't forget to dance outside too!

'Can you make a dance about a seed growing?'

'How do autumn leaves move as they fall from the trees?'

'Can you make a robot dance round the whole garden?'

LINKS TO EARLY LEARNING GOALS

EA&D	1	Exploring and using media and materials
EA&D	2	Being imaginative
PD	1	Moving and handling

Small World Toys

Lots of Small World toys are mixed up in the sand. Can you get them out without touching them?

WHAT YOU NEED

In addition to choice from the general resources:

- a trough of dry sand
- a selection of small world animals
- a selection of storage containers

WHAT YOU DO

1. Present the problem to the children using one of the suggested stimuli and discuss how to solve it. Think about all the ways they could get the animals out of the sand without touching them. Listen carefully to all their suggestions.
2. Give plenty of time for the children to select the resources.
3. Support their attempts by using scaffolding or open-ended questions to encourage their Problem Solving skills.
4. Discuss their efforts as they work, ensuring you do not solve the problem for them, or reject any of their ideas.
5. When they have finished, let the children demonstrate their ideas to each other and share comments on how the solutions worked, and which was best.

LINKS TO EARLY LEARNING GOALS

EA&D ❶ Exploring and using media and materials

PD ❶ Moving and handling

EA&D ❷ Being imaginative

USEFUL VOCABULARY

- animal
- sand
- wet
- dry
- damp
- separate
- mixed
- scoop
- sieve
- colander
- teaspoon
- tablespoon
- slotted
- ladle
- tea strainer
- tongs
- tweezers
- container

IDEAS FOR PRESENTATION

- use the template from the Problem Solving bank to write a letter from someone in the setting
- use the template from the Problem Solving bank to make a card
- record on one of the 'Talking' resources (see p75)

TAKING IT FURTHER

- Photograph the process and all the attempts, even the ones that didn't work.

Then you could:

- Add other resources to the sand to be separated:
  – paper clips, sequins, counters, coins (or a mixture)
  – large balls
  – boxes etc.
- Try it with wet sand, flour, tea leaves, cooked pasta, compost.

AND ANOTHER THING...

Mixtures are fascinating, make them part of your planning.

'All the letters of the alphabet are buried in the sand. Can you find the letters of your name?'

'Can you get the sequins out of the sand without using your hands?

Wet Sand

We need to dry the sand quickly for another activity. Can you thnk of a way to do it?

WHAT YOU NEED

In addition to choice from the general resources:

- flat trays and containers
- plenty of wet sand!

WHAT YOU DO

1. Introduce the problem and encourage the children to come up with as many ideas as they can think of. Don't reject any ideas.
2. Talk about what makes other things dry, such as the wind, a towel, a warm place.
3. Let the children decide who they want to work with.
4. Encourage them to select any resources they might need.
5. Support their attempts using scaffolding and open-ended questions. This challenge may take some time, so be patient and support the process.
6. Discuss their progress and the ideas they are exploring, making sure you do not solve the problem for them.
7. Share all their ideas and discuss which ones are best.

IDEAS FOR PRESENTATION

- a message on the sand tray
- recorded on one of the 'Talking' resources (see p75)

USEFUL VOCABULARY

In addition to choice from the general resources:

- wet
- dry
- damp
- heat
- towel
- wind
- blow
- hairdryer
- radiator
- sunshine
- cooker
- spread
- tray
- shallow
- amount

TAKING IT FURTHER

- Photograph or record all the ideas.
- Record by drawing and writing about it.

Then you could:

- Make the sand even wetter.
- Use very moist playdough and try the techniques with this.
- Put up a washing line to explore drying wet papers and fabrics.

AND ANOTHER THING...

Changing things is a problem!

'We need some grey paint and I've forgotten how to make it. Do you know how to do it?'

'What happens to sugar when you put it in water? How could you find out?'

LINKS TO EARLY LEARNING GOALS

EA&D ❶ Exploring and using media and materials

PD ❶ Moving and handling

Tall Building

Who can build the tallest sand building in the sand tray?

WHAT YOU NEED

In addition to choice from the general resources:

- measuring tapes, rulers and string
- some toy flags and flagpoles
- water and container
- pictures of tall buildings

USEFUL VOCABULARY

In addition to choice from the general resources:

- bear
- sand
- wet
- dry
- damp
- tower
- support
- inside
- outside
- height
- tall
- taller
- short
- shorter
- compare
- measure
- tape
- ruler
- string
- collapse
- crumble
- fall

WHAT YOU DO

1. Present the problem to the group of children using one of the suggested stimuli. Discuss the problem and solutions.
2. Talk about the shapes of tall buildings and look at some pictures together.
3. Let the children decide whether to work alone, in pairs or as a group.
4. Talk about wet and dry sand, and which is best for building. Let them add some water if they need it.
5. Give them time to select resources.
6. Support their attempts sensitively as they work, encouraging thinking skills without solving the problem for them.
7. Finally, let the children compare the heights of the towers and share comments about their work.

IDEAS FOR PRESENTATION

- challenge left in the sand tray
- use the template from the Problem Solving bank to make a card
- record on one of the 'Talking' resources (see p75)

TAKING IT FURTHER

- Design the structure before starting, or draw it afterwards.
- Photograph the process and the solutions.

Then you could:

- Make other tall buildings.
- Make bridges and tunnels.
- Look at some books, then use bricks and boxes to make different sorts of tall buildings.

AND ANOTHER THING...

Sand offers so many opportunities for Problem Solving.

> *'Can you move sand from one side of the room/ garden to the other without touching it?'*
>
> *'How much sand can you fit in this bucket? How could you measure it?'*

LINKS TO EARLY LEARNING GOALS

EA&D ❶ Exploring and using media and materials

M ❷ Shape, space and measures

PD&M ❶ Moving and handling

Stop the Leak!

Sometimes the juice leaks out of the cartons and makes a terrible mess. Can you think of a way to stop the leak?

WHAT YOU NEED

In addition to choice from the general resources:

- a selection of juice cartons or plastic bottles with holes
- a tool box containing a variety of tapes, scissors, string etc.
- cloths

WHAT YOU DO

1. Present the challenge to the children and discuss what they could do.
2. Explain that you are going to use water instead of juice for the experiments because of the mess and waste.
3. Let each child choose a carton or plastic milk bottle with a small hole in it.
4. Let the children select materials from the tool box to repair the leak and test it with water.
5. Support their efforts using open-ended questions (see p14) to encourage thinking and talking skills.
6. Discuss their progress as they work, encouraging them to try more ways till they find one that works.
7. Have a discussion about what works best to stop the leak.

LINKS TO EARLY LEARNING GOALS

EA&D ❶ Exploring and using media and materials
PD ❶ Moving and handling
EA&D ❷ Being imaginative

USEFUL VOCABULARY

In addition to choice from the general resources:

- water
- milk
- liquid
- carton
- bottle
- leak
- waterproof
- tape
- drip
- dribble
- run
- pour
- soak
- wet
- mess
- stop
- seal

IDEAS FOR PRESENTATION

- use the template from the Problem Solving bank to write a letter from an adult
- a message from the milkman or shop keeper
- use the template from the Problem Solving bank to make a card
- record on one of the 'Talking' resources (see p75)

TAKING IT FURTHER

- Design or draw your plan to solve the problem.
- Photograph it.

Then you could:

- Try to stop leaks from bigger holes.
- Try to stop leaks from irregular shaped containers.
- Try different sorts of tapes and other materials to stop leaks.

AND ANOTHER THING...

Water gives many opportunities for experimenting and solving problems.

'How could you make a paper boat waterproof?'

'How much water can you get in this bottle? How could you measure it?'

'How can you make things sink?'

'Do all leaves float?'

Empty the Tray

The tap on the water tray has jammed. Can you think of how we can empty the tray?

WHAT YOU NEED

In addition to choice from the general resources:

- a large variety of containers, basins and buckets
- plenty of mopping up and drying equipment!

WHAT YOU DO

1. Present the problem to the group of children and discuss how it could be solved. It might be better to do this one outside!
2. Demonstrate the 'jammed' tap.
3. Talk about things that hold water.
4. Encourage the children to experiment with the resources.
5. Support their attempts, using your skills to encourage talking and thinking.
6. As they work, discuss their progress ensuring that you do not solve the problem for them, or show too much anxiety about the spills!
7. Let the children talk about their ideas and share solutions.

TAKING IT FURTHER

- Draw a picture of what you did.
- Photograph the children at work.

Then you could:

- Remove the containers and utensils and let the children explore emptying activities using less common items such as sponges, rubber gloves, shopping bags etc.
- Explore how water wheels, tubing and funnels could be used to empty a water tray.

USEFUL VOCABULARY

In addition to choice from the general resources:

- trough
- tap
- water
- jammed
- stuck
- empty
- full
- containers
- spill
- drips

IDEAS FOR PRESENTATION

- use the template from the Problem Solving bank to make a card
- record on one of the 'Talking' resources (see p75)

AND ANOTHER THING...

Present simple problems for the children to discuss and suggest solutions to.

'This door keeps slamming in the wind. How can we stop it?'

'I have lost my gloves again! How can I find them and keep them safe?'

'The football games stop other children from playing on the patio. How can we keep everyone happy?'

LINKS TO EARLY LEARNING GOALS

EA&D ❶ Exploring and using media and materials
PD ❶ Moving and handling
EA&D ❷ Being imaginative

Pirate Treasure

The pirate have found lots of treasure. Can you make a ship out of foil to carry it?

WHAT YOU NEED

In addition to choice from the general resources:

- a selection of pictures of ships and boats
- the pirate's treasure, such as coins, jewellery, precious stones
- rolls of foil
- scissors

WHAT YOU DO

1. Talk about the problem with the children, using the pictures and objects to aid the discussion.
2. Look at some pictures of ships and boats and talk about their shapes and how they float.
3. Cut or tear some lengths of foil so the children can begin creating their ships.
4. Share out the treasure.
5. Stay near so you can support their attempts, using scaffolding and open-ended questions (see p14).
6. Discuss progress, help them to cope with false starts and structures that don't work.
7. Try floating the ships on a shallow bowl of water.

IDEAS FOR PRESENTATION

- use the template from the Problem Solving bank to write a letter from a pirate (in a bottle?)
- use the template from the Problem Solving bank to make a card
- record on one of the 'Talking' resources (see p75)

USEFUL VOCABULARY

In addition to choice from the general resources:

- pirate
- treasure
- coins
- jewellery
- precious
- stones
- diamonds
- rubies
- sapphires
- emeralds
- ship
- float
- sink
- sides
- base
- waterproof
- seal
- leak
- weight
- hold
- balance

TAKING IT FURTHER

- Design or draw the ship before starting or after it is finished.
- Photograph the boats.

Then you could:

- Explore the best containers to use in the water.
- Just use coins for the treasure, and record the number of coins added before each pirate ship sinks.

AND ANOTHER THING...

Children love making and sailing boats.

'Can you make a boat with a sail?'

'Can you make a boat from plasticine?'

'How many pieces of Lego can you float in a boat made from a plastic tray? Challenge your friends and keep score.'

'How could you make a piece of cardboard waterproof?'

LINKS TO EARLY LEARNING GOALS

EA&D ❶ Exploring and using media and materials
M ❷ Shape, space and measures
PD ❶ Moving and handling
EA&D ❷ Being imaginative

Toy Car

Can you make a toy car move without pushing or pulling it with your hands?

WHAT YOU NEED

In addition to choice from the general resources:

- a selection of toy cars
- construction kits with wheels

USEFUL VOCABULARY

- car
- move
- surface
- flat
- slope
- push
- pull
- board
- track
- road
- support
- plank
- join
- dip
- smooth
- run
- freewheel

WHAT YOU DO

1. Present the problem to the children, and see how many ways they can think of to move a car without touching it.
2. Let the children decide whether to work individually, in pairs or in groups.
3. Let them to choose (or make) a car and select any resources they need.
4. Support their attempts by using scaffolding or open-ended (see p14) questions to encourage thinking and talking skills.
5. Stay near so you can talk about their progress, ensuring you do not solve the problem for them.
6. Finally, let the children demonstrate their ideas to each other and share comments about what worked and what didn't.

TAKING IT FURTHER

- Design or draw your idea.
- Photograph the ideas that worked as well as those that didn't.

Then you could:

- Find out how to move a boat without pushing or pulling it with your hands.
- Find out how to move a ball without pushing or pulling it with your hands.

AND ANOTHER THING...

Try moving other objects without touching them.

'Can you move a piece of paper without touching it?'

'Can you get some sand to the top of the climbing frame without carrying it in your hands?'

'How do electric doors work?'

IDEAS FOR PRESENTATION

- use the template from the Problem Solving bank to make a card
- a phone call from a superhero
- record on one of the 'Talking' resources (see p75)

LINKS TO EARLY LEARNING GOALS

EA&D 1 Exploring and using media and materials
PD 2 Moving and handling
EA&D 1 Being imaginative

Beads and Balls

The plastic beads and metal balls got mixed up. Can you think of a way of separating them?

WHAT YOU NEED

In addition to choice from the general resources:

- a selection of boxes of mixed up beads and balls
- containers for the separated materials

WHAT YOU DO

1. Look at the problem and talk about how it could be solved. Value all the suggestions the children make.
2. Let the children decide who they will work with to solve the problem.
3. Give each group of children a box of the mixed up beads and balls and some empty containers.
4. Encourage them to choose any more resources they think they will need.
5. Support their attempts as they work, by encouragement and sensitive questioning, without solving the problem for them.
6. When they have finished, let the children demonstrate their ideas and talk about the different methods.

TAKING IT FURTHER

- Design or draw your solution to the problem.
- Photograph what you did.

Then you could:

- Try to separate some mixed up heavy and light objects.
- Try to separate materials which dissolve or melt from others which do not.

USEFUL VOCABULARY

- tray
- box
- container
- beads
- balls
- plastic
- metal
- float
- sink
- magnet
- magnetic
- attract
- separate

AND ANOTHER THING...

Try more experiments in mixing and separating.

'How could we make this dough sparkly and pink?'

'I've just spilt a lot of sequins in the water tray. How can we get them out?'

'This string is all in a tangle, how can we untangle it?'

IDEAS FOR PRESENTATION

- a challenge card by the mixed up resources
- use the template from the Problem Solving bank to make a card
- record on one of the 'Talking' resources (see p75)

LINKS TO EARLY LEARNING GOALS

PD 1 Moving and handling
EA&D 1 Exploring and using media and materials
EA&D 2 Being imaginative

Giant Bubbles

Can you make giant bubbles?

WHAT YOU NEED

In addition to choice from the general resources:

- individual shallow containers of pre-prepared or bought bubble mix
- jugs of water, bottles of washing-up liquid, spoons
- variety of implements, wands, pipe cleaners, wire, plastic bottles
- paper towels and bin

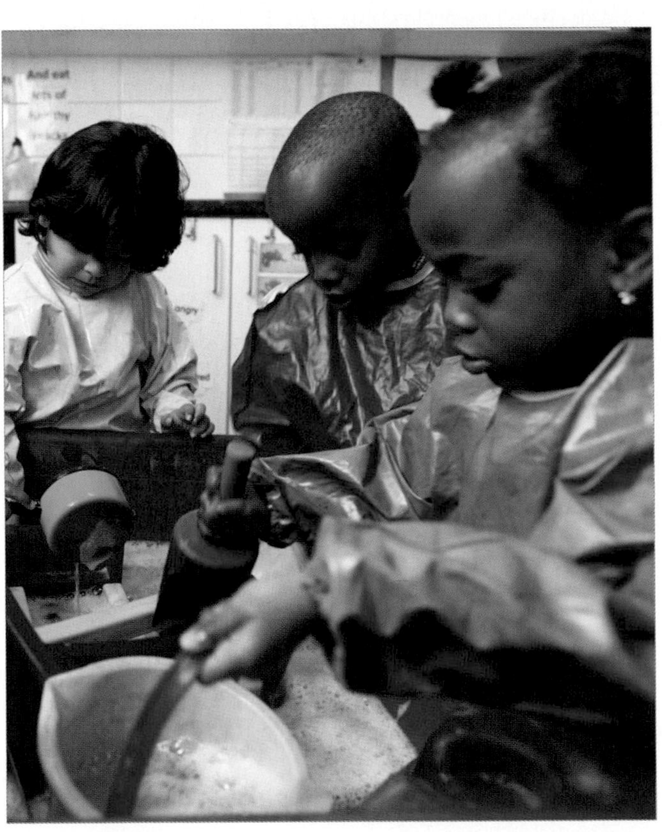

USEFUL VOCABULARY

- bubble • washing-up • liquid
- container • blow • suck • wand
- wire • tools • size • big • huge
- sphere • round • burst • float

WHAT YOU DO

1. Introduce the challenge to the children and discuss how you could make really big bubbles, and how you could measure the biggest.
2. Look at all the resources and discuss which ones might work best before leaving the children to select the ones they need.
3. Support their attempts as they work, encouraging talking and thinking.
4. Help them, if they need it, to make the 'wand-type' tools for blowing the bubbles. Discuss their progress with them, ensuring that you do not solve the problem for them.
5. Finally, let the children demonstrate their bubble blowing and share comments.

IDEAS FOR PRESENTATION

- use the template from the Problem Solving bank to make a card
- write the challenge on a piece of card suspended from a balloon above the resource

TAKING IT FURTHER

- Draw pictures.
- Photograph the activity.

Then you could:

- Try making a bubble of a different shape or colour.
- Try putting something inside a bubble.
- Explore the addition of other materials to the bubble mixture e.g. glycerine, sugar.
- Explore bubble kits and bubble machines.

AND ANOTHER THING...

Blowing bubbles outdoors can give rise to lots of interesting questions, such as:

'Why do bubbles burst?'

'What is inside a bubble?'

'How do bubbles move?'

Health & Safety – ensure the children know the difference between blowing and sucking; don't share any blowing tools they have had in their mouths; monitor the use of wire.

LINKS TO EARLY LEARNING GOALS

EA&D 1 Exploring and using media and materials

M 2 Shape, space and measures

PD 1 Moving and handling

Remote-Controlled Car

Can you invent a game for a remote-controlled car?

WHAT YOU NEED

In addition to choice from the general resources:

- clipboards, paper, mark makers, chalkboards for recording
- stop watches, sand timers

WHAT YOU DO

1. Introduce the problem to the children and discuss what needs to be done.
2. Let the children decide whether to work alone, in pairs or as a group (this may depend on the number of cars available).
3. Allow them to select a car and any other resources required.
4. Support their attempts using scaffolding and open-ended questions (see p14) to encourage thinking and talking skills.
5. Discuss their progress as they work, but try not to interfere or slow down their thinking, and ensuring you do not solve the problem for them.
6. Help with recording the rules if they need it or ask for help.
7. Let them demonstrate their games to the other children and discuss how well they work.

TAKING IT FURTHER

- Design and draw your game before starting work.
- Write down the instructions.
- Record the instructions on a Talking Tin or dictaphone.

USEFUL VOCABULARY

- aerial
- batteries
- switch
- drive
- forwards
- backwards
- left
- right
- stop
- remote-control
- obstacle
- under
- over
- round
- rules
- timer
- object

IDEAS FOR PRESENTATION

- use the template from the Problem Solving bank to make a card
- record on one of the 'Talking' resources (see p75)
- a message from someone else in the setting

Then you could:

- Invent a different game.
- Invent a game for:
  – a metal detector
  – a Bee-Bot
  – a pair of walkie-talkies.

AND ANOTHER THING...

Use your outdoor area for larger scale games and challenges, including the use of playground chalk or white boards for the instructions.

'Can you use chalk to make a treasure hunt for other children?'

'Could you make a giant snakes and ladders game?'

LINKS TO EARLY LEARNING GOALS

EA&D	2	Being imaginative
M	2	Shape, space and measures
UW	3	Technology

Mending Games

This box is full of broken toys and games. Can you help to mend them?

WHAT YOU NEED

In addition to choice from the general resources:

- a box containing a variety of broken toys (NB – ensure there are no sharp or dangerous parts)
- a 'tool box' containing scissors, string, glue, various types of tape, stapler etc.

USEFUL VOCABULARY

- mend • fix • repair • sort • plastic
- rubber • cardboard • fabric • wood
- tape • glue • string • attach
- hold • firm • fit • support • cut

WHAT YOU DO

1. Using one of the suggested stimuli, present the problem to the children and discuss.
2. Talk about the properties of the broken toys and what might be used to repair them.
3. Encourage the children to choose from the contents of the box and any resources or tools for the repairs, selecting from either the 'tool box' or from the general resources in the art and design area.
4. Support them by using scaffolding and open-ended questions (see p14) to encourage their thinking and talking skills.
5. Discuss their attempts, but make sure that you do not solve the problem for them.

TAKING IT FURTHER

- Increase the number of missing or broken parts.
- Include odd parts which don't belong.

Then you could:

- Try the same activity with torn or damaged books, household items (look for these in charity shops or jumble sales).
- Suggest that the children could bring broken toys from home to mend and fix.

AND ANOTHER THING...

Use broken or old toys and other objects to find out how things work.

'How could we fix this broken toy?'

'How does a trike work?'

IDEAS FOR PRESENTATION

- use the template from the Problem Solving bank to write a letter from someone in the setting
- use the template from the Problem Solving bank to make a card
- record on one of the 'Talking' resources (see p75)

LINKS TO EARLY LEARNING GOALS

EA&D 1 Exploring and using media and materials
PD 1 Moving and handling
UW 2 The world

Bee-Bot

Can you invent a Bee-Bot game?

WHAT YOU NEED

In addition to choice from the general resources:

- a selection of Bee-Bot mats including the transparent squared type
- large sheets of paper, plain or with same sizes of squares as the mat
- mark makers

WHAT YOU DO

1. Present the challenge to the children and discuss how to go about the task. Treat all suggestions seriously.
2. Talk about their experiences using the Bee-Bot, the games they have played and the variety of mats.
3. Let the children decide whether to work alone or in a group.
4. Look at the resources and help them to select what they need.
5. Support them as they work, using scaffolding and open-ended questions to encourage thinking and talking skills.
6. Stay near and discuss their progress, making sure you do not solve the problem for them.
7. Let them demonstrate their games to the group and invite comments from the other children.

USEFUL VOCABULARY

- Bee-Bot
- robot
- mats
- games
- programme
- square
- forward
- backward
- pause
- stop
- go
- left
- right
- shape
- number
- colour

TAKING IT FURTHER

- Design or draw the game before making it.
- Photograph the games in progress.

Then you could:

- Invent a different game.
- Invent games for other ICT resources for example:
  - a metal detector
  - a remote control car
  - a remote control bug
  - walkie talkies.

AND ANOTHER THING...

Create a large grid either indoors or out using chalks or tape. Add some colours and shapes to it and let the children pretend to be 'Bee-Bot'.

Encourage directional and numerical language in their game e.g. sideways, twice etc.

'What different ways can you move your body from one square to the next?'

IDEAS FOR PRESENTATION

- use the template from the Problem Solving bank to write a letter from Bee-Bot
- use the template from the Problem Solving bank to make a card
- record on one of the 'Talking' resources (see p75)

LINKS TO EARLY LEARNING GOALS

M	1	Numbers
M	2	Shape, space and measures
UW	3	Technology
EA&D	2	Beingimaginative

Bear Hunt 2

The children want to go on a Bear Hunt again. Can you draw them a map so they can find the same cave?

WHAT YOU NEED

In addition to choice from the general resources:

- the book 'We're all Going on a Bear Hunt' by Michael Rosen and Helen Oxenbury
- a selection of maps, plans, atlases

WHAT YOU DO

1. Introduce the problem and discuss how you could make a map. Listen to all the suggestions, and don't reject any.
2. Look at the story again, then look at maps and plans and how they help to find your way.
3. Let the children decide whether to work alone, in pairs or in a group.
4. Give them time to select the resources they need.
5. Use scaffolding and open-ended questions (see p14) as you support their thinking and talking.
6. When they are ready, let the children show and explain their maps to the others and share comments, saying which solution they like best and which ones would work.

TAKING IT FURTHER

- Photograph it.

Then you could:

- Make a 3D map of the Bear Hunt story, with mud, grass etc.
- Make a map of how you go home, go to the park, go to a friend's house, go to the shops.
- Make a map of the local area and add photographs.
- Label your maps.

USEFUL VOCABULARY

- bear
- find
- map
- plan
- atlas
- direction
- right
- left
- straight ahead
- turn
- follow
- far
- near
- forward
- hill
- grass
- river
- mud
- forest
- snowstorm
- cave

IDEAS FOR PRESENTATION

- use the template from the Problem Solving bank to write a letter from one of the children
- use the template from the Problem Solving bank to make a card
- record on one of the 'Talking' resources (see p75)

AND ANOTHER THING...

Make maps and plans together by adding them to your repertoire of Problem Solving activities.

'A visitor has just emailed and needs to know how to get to the school. Can we draw a map to help her find her way here?'

'When we go to the park for a walk, we need a map. Can you make one?'

LINKS TO EARLY LEARNING GOALS

EA&D	2	Being imaginative
M	2	Shape, space and measures
L	2	Writing
UW	2	The world

Tiny Birthday

A tiny person is having a birthday. Can you make her a tiny card and envelope?

WHAT YOU NEED

In addition to choice from the general resources:

- cards
- a variety of envelopes

WHAT YOU DO

1. Present the problem to the group of children using one of the suggested stimuli and discuss.
2. Talk about who the very small person might be, where they live, what they look like, what sort of card they might like.
3. Look at and discuss cards and envelopes.
4. Look at all the resources available and give time for the children to select what they need.
5. Stay near, or revisit frequently to support their work and develop Problem Solving skills.
6. Talk about what they are doing without distracting them, and make sure you don't solve the problem for them.
7. Give time for the children to show each other their cards and envelopes, and share comments.

TAKING IT FURTHER

- Photograph the activity in progress.

Then you could:

- Talk about how you could get the card to the very small person, where to leave it or send it.
- Make other cards and letters to send to friends or story characters.
- Make a card and envelope to send to a giant.
- Make cards for different occasions such as Eid, invitations, Thank You, Diwali.

USEFUL VOCABULARY

- pixie
- birthday
- tiny
- small
- card
- fold
- envelope
- shape
- join
- glue
- staple
- stamp
- name
- address
- post
- collection

IDEAS FOR PRESENTATION

- use the template from the Problem Solving bank to write a letter from a small person
- use the template from the Problem Solving bank to make a card
- record on one of the 'Talking' resources (see p75)

AND ANOTHER THING...

Make sure there are plenty of mark-making resources indoors and outside for making signs, card and messages.

'Can you make a sign to warn children that the slide is broken?'

'The mums and dads are coming to assembly tomorrow. Can you make a notice that tells them where to go?'

'I've just found this letter in the garden. I wonder what it says?'

LINKS TO EARLY LEARNING GOALS

EA&D 1 Exploring and using media and materials

EA&D 2 Being imaginative

PD 1 Moving and handling

Lunch Menu

Can you make a lunch menu for the Home Corner Café?

WHAT YOU NEED

In addition to the available resources:

- examples of menus
- a selection of menu holders

WHAT YOU DO

1. Using one of the suggested stimuli, present the problem to the children and discuss.
2. Look at the examples of menus and discuss the contents.
3. Allow them to decide whether to work alone or in pairs.
4. Give them time to select the resources they need.
5. As they work, support their attempts using scaffolding and open-ended questions (see p14).
6. Let them show and read the menu list and prices to the other children.

IDEAS FOR PRESENTATION

- use the template from the Problem Solving bank to make a card
- recorded on one of the 'Talking' resources (see p75)

USEFUL VOCABULARY

- menu
- holder
- card
- list
- column
- food
- price
- each
- eat
- drink
- packet
- hot
- cold
- fresh

TAKING IT FURTHER

- Photograph the process.
- Decorate the menu.
- Make menus for different situations e.g. restaurants of other cultures, parties.

LINKS TO EARLY LEARNING GOALS

L ❷ Writing
PD ❶ Moving and handling
EA&D ❷ Being imaginative

AND ANOTHER THING...

Use writing and graphics across the curriculum e.g. to plan a construction; to make notices for the setting; in role play, both indoors and out.

'Can you make labels for the storage boxes?'

'Can you make a plan of the setting?'

'Can you make price tags for the Home Corner shop?'

Bird House

A little bird's house blew away. Can you make/build a new house for it using things you find in the garden?

USEFUL VOCABULARY

- bird • tiny • house • nest • grass
- twig • leaves • branch • flower
- feather • tree • weave • door
- attach • fasten • tie • hang • hide

WHAT YOU NEED

In addition to choice from the general resources:

- selection of toy birds
- access to a range of safe natural materials such as feathers, sticks, grass, hay, leaves
- bird books

IDEAS FOR PRESENTATION

- use the template from the Problem Solving bank to write a letter left outside from a bird with no nest
- a bird puppet with a label round its neck
- record on one of the 'Talking' resources (see p75)

WHAT YOU DO

1. Introduce the problem to the children using one of the suggested stimuli.
2. Talk about birds and where they like to live.
3. Let the children decide whether to work alone, in pairs or as a group.
4. Let them select a toy bird, choose where to build the bird house or nest and collect the natural materials.
5. Watch as they work, support their attempts using scaffolding and open-ended questions (see p14) to encourage thinking and talking.
6. Discuss and help with fastenings if they need it, taking care that you do not solve the problem for them.
7. Let everyone show their efforts and share comments about how they solved the problem.

LINKS TO EARLY LEARNING GOALS

EA&D ① Exploring and using media and materials
EA&D ② Being imaginative
PD ① Moving and handling

TAKING IT FURTHER

- Design or draw the bird house before starting work.
- Take a photograph of the processes and the products of the Problem Solving.

Then you could:

- Make or build a house for a:
  - mouse
  - hedgehog
  - ladybird
  - snake.

AND ANOTHER THING...

Use natural materials indoors and outside to explore Problem Solving.

'Can you sort these sticks out into different groups?'

'How can you find out which tree these leaves came from?'

'How many stones will fit in this bucket?'

Game for this Picture

Can you invent a game for this picture?

WHAT YOU NEED

In addition to choice from the general resources:

- playground paint, or chalk if it is not to be permanent
- a picture, grid, resources or shapes as a base for the game
- clipboards, paper and mark-makers to record rules

WHAT YOU DO

1. Introduce the challenge and collect ideas from the children of how the game could be made.
2. Talk about outdoor games and indoor board games they have played before.
3. Allow the children to choose to work alone, in pairs or groups.
4. Support their attempts using open-ended questions (see p14) that will encourage thinking and talking skills.
5. Support the children in recording the rules for their game if they need it or ask you to.
6. Take all their efforts seriously and don't take over.
7. Make time for the children to demonstrate their games to the other children and listen to their comments.

USEFUL VOCABULARY

- game
- indoors
- outdoors
- board
- base
- rules
- object
- players
- moves
- turns
- winner
- points
- lines

IDEAS FOR PRESENTATION

- use the template from the Problem Solving bank to make a card
- record on one of the 'Talking' resources (see p75)

TAKING IT FURTHER

- Draw the game.
- Record the rules on one of the 'Talking' resources (see p75).

Then you could:

- Make up other games using different bases or pictures.

AND ANOTHER THING...

Making games is fun for most children and gives them plenty of number practice.

'Can you use the numbers from junk mail to make a counting game?'

'Here are some number stamps or stickers. Can you use them to make a game?'

'How can we make a fishing game with the boats in the water tray?'

'Who can jump furthest? How could we find out?'

LINKS TO EARLY LEARNING GOALS

EA&D	2	Being imaginative
PD	1	Moving and handling
M1	1	Numbers

Make a Den!

Can you make a den for two children to hide in?

USEFUL VOCABULARY

- fabric
- material
- rope
- support
- pole
- base
- attach
- fix
- tie
- doorway
- flap
- sag
- strong
- hold
- peg
- clip

WHAT YOU NEED

In addition to choice from the general resources:

- sticks, canes
- fastening materials such as string, cable ties
- materials to make signs for the front of the den

WHAT YOU DO

1. Introduce the problem and talk about it together, discussing different sorts of dens, tents and shelters. Encourage children to offer their ideas for construction, coverings etc.
2. Let the children decide whether to work alone or as a group.
3. Visit your construction area, look at all the resources, including the ones that are new. Give plenty of time for children to look at and select the resources they need.
4. Support their work using open-ended questions (see p14) to encourage thinking and Problem Solving skills.
5. Discuss their progress with them, ensuring that you do not solve the problem for them.
6. Visit all the dens and talk about them together.

TAKING IT FURTHER

- Design or draw your idea before you start.
- Photograph the dens, during the construction and after, when they are being used by the children.

Then you could:

- Make something for four children to hide in.
- Make a circus tent.
- Make bird watchers' hide.
- Make a shelter for a wet day.
- Make a tent for a superhero figure, soft toy or small world character.

AND ANOTHER THING...

Outdoors is a great place to make dens, but don't forget some children like to make dens indoors too!

'Where could we put this big box, so children can get inside it?'

'How can we make somewhere dark?'

IDEAS FOR PRESENTATION

- a challenge card hanging from a tree, fence or bush
- record on one of the 'Talking' resources (see p75)

LINKS TO EARLY LEARNING GOALS

EA&D 1 Exploring and using media and materials
PD 1 Moving and handling
EA&D 2 Being imaginative

Waterway

Can you build a waterway that the boat can sail across?

WHAT YOU NEED

In addition to choice from the general resources:

- access to water – a tap, hosepipe or large container
- a variety of containers, watering cans, jugs
- a tool box containing a selection of tapes, scissors, string, rope
- waterproof aprons or overalls
- paper towels and bin
- selection of small boats

WHAT YOU DO

1. Present the problem to the children, listening to their ideas and encouraging them to think of different ways to solve it.
2. Talk about ways of creating a long waterway, including ways to fix materials together and support the waterway.
3. Help them to decide whether to work alone, in pairs or as a group (this could be influenced by the number and selection of available resources).
4. Allow the children to select their resources.
5. Support their attempts to encourage their thinking and talking.
6. Discuss their progress with them, ensuring that you do not solve the problem for them.
7. Let them demonstrate their waterways and talk about them.

USEFUL VOCABULARY

- boat
- sail
- distance
- water
- channel
- pipes
- gutters
- tubes
- stands
- support
- raise
- attach
- string
- rope
- Velcro
- slope
- leak
- drip
- tape
- waterproof

TAKING IT FURTHER

- Design or draw your idea before starting.
- Photograph the process of solving the problem as well as the solution.

Then you could:

- Make adjustments to the waterways to make the boats sail faster or slower.
- Make the channel longer or shorter.
- Make a boat to sail in it, or explore what else can float.
- Try moving dry sand down the waterway.

AND ANOTHER THING...

Use natural materials for challenges indoors.

'Can you make a pattern with these stones?'

'Could you make a raft for this man, using wood and string?'

'How can you make these leaves into a picture?

IDEAS FOR PRESENTATION

- use the template from the Problem Solving bank to make a card
- record on one of the 'Talking' resources (see p75)
- use the template from the Problem Solving bank to write a letter left outside near the tap

LINKS TO EARLY LEARNING GOALS

EA&D 1 Exploring and using media and materials
PD 1 Moving and handling
EA&D 2 Being imaginative

Teddy Cool

It is very hot and sunny outside today. Can you build a shelter for Teddy to keep him cool?

WHAT YOU NEED

In addition to choice from the general resources:

- steddy bears or other soft toys
- den building and outdoor open-ended construction materials

WHAT YOU DO

1. Using one of the suggested stimuli, present the problem to the group. Think about and discuss all the solutions the children can think of.
2. Talk about the effects of the sun and how it can be harmful.
3. Let the children decide who they would like to work with.
4. Look at the resources and give time for the children to select what they need.
5. Support them as they work, using your skills to encourage their thinking and talking skills for Problem Solving.
6. Be available to discuss their work in progress, but don't solve the problem for them.
7. Finally, arrange a session when the children can show their shelters to each other and share comments.

LINKS TO EARLY LEARNING GOALS

EA&D ① Exploring and using media and materials
EA&D ② Being imaginative
PD ① Moving and handling

USEFUL VOCABULARY

- bird
- weather
- light
- sun
- shade
- shadow
- fix
- fasten
- attach
- support
- fabric
- material
- blackout
- peg
- clip
- rope
- string

IDEAS FOR PRESENTATION

- use the template from the Problem Solving bank to write a letter from Teddy
- use the template from the Problem Solving bank to make a card
- record on one of the 'Talking' resources (see p75)

TAKING IT FURTHER

- Design the shelter before you start or draw the finished shelter.
- Photograph all the shelters.

Then you could:

- Enlarge it to hold one child or more.
- Make other shelters suitable for wet, windy, cold or foggy weather.

AND ANOTHER THING...

Use woodwork, construction and mark-making to encourage Problem Solving.

'Can you make a pair of shoes from boxes?'
'This soft toy is cold. Can you make her a coat?'
'How can you fix wood together without using nails?'
'Can you make a tent with a window?'
'Can you make a pair of sunglasses?'
'Can you make a box for this present?'

'TALKING' RESOURCES FOR RECORDING MESSAGES ANG CHALLENGES

From www.tts-group.co.uk –

RECORDABLE POSTCARDS
Display your own picture or photograph in the plastic window provided and record some information about it (up to 10 seconds)

Write-on/wipe-off

TALKING PHOTO ALBUMS
Insert drawings or photographs into the plastic wallets and record up to a 10 second message on every page to support the image or text.

Holds 24 inserts of 6"x4"

Available in sizes A3, A4, A5

RECORDABLE PEGS
Set includes 6 recordable pegs in 6 bright colours

10 seconds recording time

Clips on or attaches magnetically

RAINBOW TALKING BOXES
A selection of differently coloured boxes which can be used to record a message which will play back on opening the box

10 seconds recording time

TALK-POINT
10 seconds recording time version is available in 5 colours

30 seconds version is black

TALK-TIME POSTCARDS and RAINBOW TALK-TIME CARDS
A6 cards are write-on/wipe-off with a clear plastic pocket to insert own cards

10 seconds recording time

RAINBOW TALKING BOXES
Made from heavy gauge card and activated by light sensors when opened

10 seconds recording time

RECORDABLE THOUGHT CLOUDS and SPEECH BUBBLES
10 seconds recording time

Write-on/wipe-off using dry wipe markers
From www.TalkingProducts.com –

TALKING TINS
Yellow tin has 10 seconds recording time; red tin has 40 seconds

Has built-in magnet for attachment to any metal surface

RECORDABLE GREETING CARDS
Can be decorated

Available in 10 seconds or 40 seconds recording time

VOICE PADS
10 seconds recording time

TALKING LABELS
20 seconds recording time

FURTHER READING

Ashman, A and Conway, R; Using Cognitive Methods in the Classroom; Routledge 1992
978 – 0415068369

Brown, S and Walker, M; The Art of Problem Posing; Lawrence Erlbaum 2004
978 – 0805849776

Burden, R and Williams, M; Thinking through the Curriculum; Routledge Falmer 1998
978 – 0415172028

Call, N with Featherstone, S; The Thinking Child; Network Educational Press/Continuum 2003
978 – 1855391215

Costello, P; Thinking Skills and Early Childhood Education, Early Years and Primary; Fulton 2006
978 – 1853465512

De Boo, M; Science 3 – 6 : Laying the Foundations in the Early Years; Association for Science Education 1999
978 – 0863573088

Edwards, S; Problem Solving (Skills for Early Years); Scholastic 2001
978 – 0439019125

Fisher, R; Problem Solving in Primary Schools; Blackwell 1987
978 – 0631901457

Fisher, R; Teaching Children to Think; Nelson Thornes 2005
978 – 0748794416

Hohmann, M and Weikart, D; Educating Young Children; High/Scope Press 2002
978 – 1573791045

Nutbrown, C; Threads of Thinking; Paul Chapman 2006
978 – 1412910842

Siraj – Blatchford, I and MacLeod – Brunell, I; Supporting Science, Design and Technology in the Early Years; Open University Press 1999
978 – 0335199426

Stevenson, R and Palmer, J; Learning : Principles, Processes and Practices; Continuum International 1994
978 – 0304325634

Wallace, B (ed.); Teaching Thinking Skills Across the Early Years: A Practical Approach 4 – 7; NACE/Fulton 2002
978 – 185346842

STORIES AND POEMS

We're all going on a Bear Hunt; Rosen, M and Oxenbury, H; Walker Books 1993.
978 – 0744523232

For a selection of songs, poems and rhymes – This Little Puffin; Matterson, E ed. Puffin Books 1970.
978 – 0140303001

In the Dark, Dark Wood (Lift the flap), Jessica Souhami, Francis Lincoln Children's Books 2007, ISBN – 10:1845077555 or 13:978-1845077556

In the Dark, Dark Wood

In the dark, dark wood
There was a dark, dark house,
And in that dark, dark house
There was a dark, dark room,
And in that dark, dark room
There was a dark, dark cupboard,
And in that dark, dark cupboard
There was a dark, dark shelf,
And on that dark, dark shelf
There was a dark, dark box,
And in that dark, dark box
There was a !

The poem 'In the Dark, Dark Wood' relates to the activity on p40.

SUPPLIERS AND RESOURCES

ASCO – www.ascoeducational.co.uk

Construct-a-Space Playhouse Frames; Edra Giant Construction; Link Kits; Alti System

COMMUNITY PLAYTHINGS – www.CommunityPlaythings.co.uk

Hollow Blocks and Mini Hollow Blocks; Unit Blocks and Mini Unit Blocks; Wheelbarrows

MINDSTRETCHERS – www.mindstretchers.co.uk

Bark Blocks; Treehouse Kits; Mini Logs (Creative Blocks); Bamboo Guttering Sets; Camouflage Nets; Den Building Kits; Playstands; Play Fabrics; Velcro Straps; Hemp and Nylon Ropes; Tarps and Waterproof Sheets; Block and Tackle Sets; Talking Tubs;

Planning resources – Talkaround Mats; Talking and Thinking Floorbooks; Talking and Thinking Trees; Talk About Mats

TTS – www.tts-group.co.uk

Camouflage Den Making Set; Creative Cascade Set; Giant Obstacle Course; Weaving Frames and Room Dividers

TTS – ICT resources – e.g. Karaoke Machine; Voice Changer; Bee-Bot; Remote Controlled Vehicles; Make'n'Go; Metal Detector

QUADRO – www.quadroplay.co.uk

Giant Quadro Construction

SPECTRUM – www.spectrumeducational.co.uk

Bauplay Construction

WESCO – www.wescona.com

Alfresco Blocks; Scogym

DIY STORES

Plumbing resources – plastic pipes, corner bends, u bends, guttering, joints, flexible tubes etc; wheels, castors, wooden poles, clips, pegs

EXAMPLE OF A TEMPLATE FOR A LETTER

A variety of fonts, both computer-generated and hand-written should be used in the letters to give children the experience of seeing different types of print.

Including a picture will provide added stimulus and act as a visual reference point while the children are working, but ensure that its contents do not help to solve the problem for them.

Using a large stamped envelope addressed to the children who can then open it, will add to the fun.

Dear boys and girls,
This little boy is feeling very sad.
Can you make up a funny story to make him laugh?
Thank you.
From
Sally

EXAMPLE OF A TEMPLATE FOR A CARD

A variety of fonts, both computer-generated and hand-written should be used in the cards to give children the experience of seeing different types of print.

Including a picture will provide added stimulus and act as a visual reference point while the children are working, but ensure that its contents do not help solve the problem for them.

The cards can then be laminated before adding to the bank, bags or boxes.

The pirates have found buried treasure!
There are lots of gold and silver coins and jewellery.
Can you make a pirate ship out of tinfoil that can carry the treasure?

EXAMPLE OF A PLANNING/RECORDING GRID FOR PROBLEM SOLVING ACTIVITIES

Space has been left in the 'ACTIVITY' column to add others, either from suggestions given at the end of each activity, ideas from the children or your own. An additional column could be added to include comments.

TERM: YEAR:

AREA	ACTIVITY	WEEK BEGINNING											
ART/DESIGN	make bag												
	scary mask												
	castle												
	etc.												
COMMUNICATION AND LANGUAGE	sounds for 'Bear Hunt'												
	funny story												
	etc.												
CONSTRUCTION	buggy that can move 1 child												
	giraffe house												
	etc.												
MATHEMATICS	divide birthday cake												
	make a shape person												
	etc.												
MUSIC/SOUND MAKING	happy music												
	etc.												